one

From Glenn

AMERICA'S HISTORIC HOUSES
The Living Past

AMERICA'S

HISTORIC HOUSES
The Living Past

BY THE EDITORS OF COUNTRY BEAUTIFUL

EDITORIAL DIRECTION: MICHAEL P. DINEEN
EDITED BY ROBERT L. POLLEY
MANAGING EDITOR: CHARLES R. FOWLER

Published by Country Beautiful Corporation
Waukesha, Wisconsin 53186

COUNTRY BEAUTIFUL:

Publisher and Editorial Director: *Michael P. Dineen;* Executive Editor: *Robert L. Polley;* Managing Editor: *Charles R. Fowler;* Senior Editors: *Kenneth L. Schmitz, James H. Robb;* Associate Art Director (Design): *Pricilla Unverzagt;* Associate Art Director (Production): *William M. Dichtl;* Associate Editor: *Dorothy Hennessy;* Contributing Editors: *Peter Barnicle, John W. Forssen, Maureen Bunyan;* Director of Marketing: *Mel Rozier;* Production Director: *John Dineen;* Administrative Assistant: *Sharon G. Armao;* Finance Assistant: *Trudy Schnittka;* Marketing Assistant: *Kathleen Kons;* Production Secretary: *Marlene Yogerst;* Editorial Secretary: *Gayle Butzek;* Distribution Director: *Arthur Meuler;* Production Assistant: *Lynn Simonson.*

The Editors are grateful to The Macmillan Company for permission to include the excerpts from THE MEMOIRS OF HERBERT HOOVER in the article on the Herbert Hoover Birthplace Cottage. Reprinted with permission of The Macmillan Company from THE MEMOIRS OF HERBERT HOOVER: The Years of Adventure (1874-1920). Copyright 1951 by Herbert Hoover.

Country Beautiful Corporation is a wholly owned subsidiary of Flick-Reedy Corporation: President: Frank Flick; Vice President and General Manager: Michael P. Dineen; Treasurer and Secretary: August Caamano.

Title Page: (Upper) Entrance hall of the Owens-Thomas House. (Lower) Exterior of Monticello.

CONTENTS

III SOUTHERN HOUSES

IV MIDWESTERN HOUSES

V WESTERN HOUSES

INTRODUCTION

Americans have long been fascinated by their history, perhaps partly because the nation is young enough to have so much of it still accessible. Compared to the older nations of the earth, we have a wealth of documents, pictorial material, structures and objects going back to the earliest European settlements — the English and French in the Northeast and Midwest and the Spanish in the South and Southwest.

Of this material probably nothing can bring our past so vividly back to life as the buildings wherein our forefathers dwelled. More than the plaques and monuments and forts and great public edifices, the historic houses — where Americans lived and ate, slept and discussed, wrote and dreamed, faced death and gave birth — that are still with us can recapture the essence of the past as perhaps nothing else. The only requirements are that the place has been carefully and authentically maintained, refurbished or restored and that some guidance is available.

It is the purpose of this book to provide some of that guidance for those historic houses included in this book, which leads to the question: Which houses have been included, and why?

For many decades in this country, history was thought to be concerned only with political and military people and events, and houses connected with these facets of our history are covered in this book. Many Presidents' homes and the residences of Stephen Decatur, Kit Carson, Robert E. Lee and others are here. But there is more to American history than statesmen and generals, as eminent as many of them have been. There are also our authors and architects, our social reformers and merchants, our lawyers, farmers and clergymen. The Vanderbilts, Jane Addams and Mark Twain are a vital part of the diversity that is our past. Still other houses — such as the Landis Farmhouse in Pennsylvania and the Hancock Shaker Village in Massachusetts, which are not associated with any single noteworthy person — are included because they represent a meaningful way of life during a certain period of our history.

At the same time, because of the wealth of material, it would require more than one volume to include all the houses worthy of inclusion in this book. Those that have been included represent every region of the United States in approximate proportion to the length and depth of its history, from the early 17th century, when the site of the "Oldest House" in St. Augustine was first occupied, to 1892, when Marble House in Newport, Rhode Island, was completed.

The history of the 20th century is also represented by such men as Theodore and Franklin D. Roosevelt, Herbert Hoover, Dwight D. Eisenhower and William Faulkner. For, even though the houses in this volume which were connected with their lives were built several decades before 1900, the main thrust of the impact of these men on our history was in the current century.

Considering what has been preserved for us today, it is interesting to realize how close we came to losing much of it, and we would have lost a great deal of it, had it not been for the dedicated few who saw the value of historic preservation. Beautiful Mount Vernon, probably second only to the White House in the significance of its historical associations, came frightfully close to being one of the many famous residences not to survive into our own day. Washington's fine estate was on the verge of crumbling into decay in 1853 when a persistent South Carolinian named Ann Pamela Cunningham made her first appeal to save the place. Twenty-one years later she retired from this task with the satisfaction that she had been successful.

But while it is obvious enough that such grand houses as Mount Vernon and Tryon Palace in North Carolina must be included in this book, and that such unique dwellings as the ancient Fairbanks House in Dedham, Massachusetts, and the equally old Adam Thoroughgood House in Virginia Beach, Virginia, should be covered — what about such humble abodes as the Walt Whitman House in Camden, New Jersey, and the Carry Nation House in Medicine Lodge, Kansas? The answer is that these places of unspectacular appearance are as indicative of the qualities of the historically important people who lived in them as Monticello is of the genius of Thomas Jefferson. Beautiful places and things abound in this book, but we hope this book also will convey something of the heterogeneity of the personalities involved in our nation's living past. Only then will the greatness of our history be understood and this book's purpose accomplished.

— ROBERT L. POLLEY

FAIRBANKS HOUSE
DEDHAM, MASSACHUSETTS

A House of Many Generations

The Fairbanks House in Dedham, Massachusetts, built by Jonathan Fayerbanke in 1636, is acknowledged to be the oldest wood-frame dwelling in the nation. The clapboards are weathered dark brown, as might be expected, and the venerable roof sags a bit under the weight of its years, but the house stands as it did when the first of the Fairbanks lived there back in the 17th century.

From the time of its construction up until 1903 it housed eight generations of the Fairbanks family. At the latter date the "Fairbanks Family in America" was created to maintain the old homestead.

Jonathan Fayerbanke came to the Massachusetts Bay Colony aboard the *Griffin* in 1633. With him were his wife and six children and a goodly supply of timbers and rose-colored brick from his native Yorkshire, where he probably had been a wool merchant.

In 1636 he received a grant of 16 acres in a small community then known as "Contentment," now Dedham. There were 12 acres for the growing of flax and four of swamp. With his family he set out in a canoe and made his way along the Charles River to his holdings.

With the aid of his sons, John and George, he built a six-room house on a slight knoll. He un-doubtedly had help from some of the many ships' carpenters in and around Boston. The kitchen walls show rare lapstreak paneling and there are ships' beams in the ceiling.

As was the custom in the 17th century, the house faces south. In 1648, when son John married, a wing was added, and six years later another extension, the last, was put on. The main house has a pitched roof with the north side sloping almost to the ground. The wings both have gambrel-type roofs.

The kitchen is fascinating with its great chimney of old rose-brick and a fireplace that was, in its original state, 10 feet deep and 8 feet across. The rooms are small by today's standards and the ceilings are low by any standards.

In the "milk and work room" Jonathan's ox-saddle and hay-fork are still preserved. In the parlor there is a very old piano and a case of pink rose-bordered china brought here in sailing ships. One of the bedrooms has wallpaper dating from 1850.

Since the Fairbanks Family Association was set up, the members of the family, which now number more than 600 spread across the country, have brought back many of the memorabilia carried away by some member moving west. The house is

Fairbanks House: 511 East Street, Dedham Massachusetts. Open to the public.

Above: The fireplace in the Fairbanks House kitchen was once ten feet deep and eight feet across, set in lapstreak-paneled walls. Below: Stained by age and weather, the exterior of the house is typical of early colonial design.

filled with beds, chairs, cabinets, desks, kitchen utensils, garden tools, paintings and old maps of a by-gone era — not to mention a group of cradles, one of which is said to have been used by 47 babies.

The house was built beside an old Indian trail and Jonathan, being a cautious man, built an underground tunnel which leads from the house to a meadow several yards from the house. In later years, however, the Indians became more friendly and it is well known that they used to come to the house at night and sit on the kitchen floor smoking their pipes.

But possibly the Fairbanks, being good Yankees, are proudest of the fact that throughout its more than 330 years the house has never had a mortgage encumbrance on it.

HENRY WHITFIELD HOUSE
GUILFORD, CONNECTICUT

Church, Meeting House, Hostel, Home

In July 1639 the Reverend Henry Whitfield led a group of 25 families from Surrey and Kent, England, into the American wilderness to escape the persecution of the Puritan and Separatist sects by King Charles I. The Reverend Whitfield and his group landed at Quinnipiac, now known as New Haven. The new settlers chose to move on to Menunkatuck, now Guilford, Connecticut.

They made their way from Quinnipiac to Menunkatuck in October of that year to take over land they had purchased from the Menunkatuck Indians. It is not known whether they followed an Indian trail or moved their belongings by water. In any case, they had with them some "little red cattle" given by Lady Fenwick of Saybrook and said to be among the first cattle in America.

The New England autumn with all its glories of red and gold foliage was around them, foretelling of the winter just ahead. The new colonists had little time to start many permanent dwellings, but they finished half the cellar and the Great Hall of the Reverend Whitfield's house. The following year the rest of the house was completed.

Although there was plenty of wood in the area, the colonists built the type of structure they were familiar with in Kent and Surrey; stone from a nearby ledge was used, and tradition had it that Indians helped in carting the stone by hand-barrow to the site. Mortar was made of yellow clay and oyster shells. With an abundance of material at hand the walls were made two feet thick, the beams were hand-hewn oaken timbers, and the inside partitions were wide planks of pine or whitewood joined with feathered edges.

The Great Hall is 33 feet long and 15 feet wide with a fireplace at each end. In the middle of the hall is a partition hinged to a second-floor joist that divides the room in two or swings up to the ceiling to make one large room or hall. A kitchen in an ell was added several years later.

A separate stair-tower, opening from the back of the hall, winds up to the chamber over the kitchen. There are two other chambers directly over the Great Hall. They are separated by a stairway to the garret which is a wide-open space. About one-third of the present building is original.

In its early years the house served as a home for the Reverend Whitfield, his wife Dorothy, and seven of their nine children. However, it was first of all the church, second a town meeting hall and hostel for wayfarers and lastly a home.

Whitfield returned to England in the early 1650's, but the reasons for his departure from the colony he founded are not known. He died in 1657 and is buried in Winchester. In 1659 Dorothy Whitfield returned to England where she died in 1669.

Henry Whitfield House: Whitfield Street, Guilford, Connecticut. Open to the public.

Above: The Whitfield House may be the oldest stone-house in the country, styled after the English Midlands manors of the 16th and 17th centuries. Despite the availability of other materials, tradition dictated the use of quarried stone blocks.

PAUL REVERE HOUSE
BOSTON, MASSACHUSETTS

House of a Silversmith

On the evening of December 16, 1773, Paul Revere left his home at 19 North Square in Boston and joined the throngs headed towards the Old South Meeting House to hear the decision of Governor Thomas Hutchinson regarding three ships loaded with tea which lay at Griffins Wharf. The governor insisted the tea be unloaded and the tax paid.

Suddenly a group of "Indians" appeared and with a war-whoop shouted the call. All hands went racing down to the waterfront and in a few hours some 342 chests of tea were floating out on the tide.

At dawn Paul Revere was in the saddle racing towards New York and Philadelphia with the news and a request for support. If he was like other express couriers of his day he probably paused to read the letters and pass the word along at each village and town through which he passed.

Paul Revere lived long before the days of specialization. Still considered one of the nation's greatest silversmiths, he also made eyeglasses and false-teeth that were "not only an ornament, but of real use in speaking and eating." He manufactured all

Paul Revere House: 19 North Square, Boston, Massachusetts. Open to the public.

13

the copper trim for the frigate *Constitution* ("Old Ironsides") and he roofed the Bulfinch dome of the Massachusetts State House in copper before the gold-lead was laid on.

Despite all this his greatest claim to fame, as any schoolboy will tell you, was his famous "midnight ride" on the 18th of April 1775. Henry Wadsworth Longfellow's dramatic version of how "the fate of a nation was riding that night" took some license with the facts of history.

Revere had been a member of the inner circle of the Sons of Liberty long before that warm April night when he galloped over the roads towards Lexington with the news, "The British are coming!" He spent many an evening in the parlor of the "Salutation" Tavern with other members of the North Caucus listening to John Adams, James Otis, Dr. Joseph Warren and the always present, but sometimes silent Sam Adams.

Rachel Revere gave birth to her first child at the North Square house on December 7, 1774. Undoubtedly the father was delighted, but it did not slow his work for the Sons of Liberty.

A week after the birth he was on the road again — this time headed toward Portsmouth, New Hampshire, to warn the people of that colony that General Gage was planning to send troops by sea to strengthen Fort William and Mary against possible seizure by the local militia. The same night the militia attacked the fort and captured 97 kegs of powder and more than 100 small arms. The following morning Revere was on his way back to Boston over snowy roads.

After that night's work, Revere was a marked man. He confined himself to his silversmithing, but still attended meetings of the Sons of Liberty and was kept informed of plans ahead. He could keep aware of many movements from his own home. Major Pitcairn, one of the British commanders was billeted in the house of a neighbor. British marines were located in other houses around the old square.

For many years Revere had lived in a house owned by a Dr. Clark, but in 1770 he purchased the house in North Square (which is actually a

Below: The Paul Revere House was nearly 100 years old when the famed colonial patriot purchased it in 1770. It is believed to be the oldest wood-frame house in urban America and is the point from which the celebrated "midnight ride" began in 1775.

Samuel Chamberlain

triangle). The house was nearly 100 years old when Revere purchased it, and is believed to be the oldest wooden frame house of its kind in any urban district in the country.

As far as is known, during Revere's occupancy it was always a three-story frame dwelling with an ell at the rear, and a medieval looking over-hang at the first level. During the 17th century it was a two-story dwelling and it was given its original configuration at the time of its restoration in the 20th century.

After Revere left the house in 1800, it underwent a series of changes, including the installation of a sotre-front on the first floor. The restoration was carried out in the early part of this century.

It was from this house that Paul Revere ventured forth on Sunday, April 15, 1775, before dawn, crossed the river by rowboat to Charlestown, and rode to Lexington to warn Sam Adams and John Hancock that things were afoot in Boston and they should seek a hiding place.

Three nights later all Boston knew the British were mounting an expedition to move out of the town — and the stores at Concord and the persons of Adams and Hancock seemed the most likely targets. Revere did not need the two lanterns in the steeple of the Old North Church. He knew even before he left the Boston shore that the troops were headed for the lower part of the Common to move "by sea."

His ride that night of April 18, coupled with those of Thomas Dawes and Captain Prescott, aroused the Minutemen throughout every "Middlesex village and farm." It enabled Adams and Hancock to move to safety and gave the militia at Concord time to secret their precious supplies — supplies which would come in handy at the upcoming Battle of Bunker Hill.

In 1908, the Paul Revere Memorial Association purchased and restored the old house, opening it to the public during the same year as a tribute to the true hero of Longfellow's poem.

Below: A rear view of the Paul Revere House reveals in detail colonial concepts which pervaded American architecture throughout the Revolutionary period. The over-hang of the second story is deeply rooted in the designs of medieval Europe.

HOUSE OF SEVEN GABLES
DERBY HOUSE
PEIRCE-NICHOLS HOUSE

SALEM, MASSACHUSETTS

The Richness That is Salem's History

Salem was founded in 1626 by Roger Conant, and those who joined him in the colony, then known as Naumkeag, immediately saw the economic advantages to be gained from the sea.

At first it was fishing and short trips to other colonies springing up along the New England coast. By the middle of the 18th century the sailing ships of Salem were to be found in the ports of the West Indies and after the Revolution the house-flags of Salem merchants fluttered in anchorages in Spain and Portugal and throughout the Mediterranean. It was they who opened the trade routes to Africa, China and the East Indies.

And as the trade grew and the town prospered the merchants built themselves homes in keeping with their status in the community. As a result, examples of architecture from the 17th century through the Federal period can be found in the once thriving center of world trade.

The most famous, although not the oldest, of the 17th-century houses in Salem is the "House of the Seven Gables" immortalized by Nathaniel Hawthorne in his book of that name. Actually, there is considerable doubt that the author was using the house as his model although he was well acquainted with it, since it was owned by a Miss Susan Ingersoll, a cousin, whom he visited often.

The house was built in 1668 by John Turner, a mariner and merchant. It stands at the edge of Salem Harbor where Turner could watch the ships as they came and went. Over the centuries howling nor'easters slashing in from the Atlantic have turned the house almost black.

The "cent shop" where Hepzibah sold her wares, as described in the 19th-century romance, is now the entrance used by visitors. The pine-paneled kitchen looks out on the street and a huge fireplace with a myriad of utensils is the center of attraction.

A narrow passage leads around the great center chimney to a paneled banquet room with its fine old-time furnishings. Windsor chairs are set about the long, rope-legged Sheraton table. A painting of a sailing vessel hangs over the Hepplewhite sideboard and Chinese Chippendale wallpaper is a reminder of the adventurous mariners who once occupied the house.

On either side of the fireplace is a closet. Pieces of pewter, Bristol and china ware are displayed in the one on the right. To a casual observer the one on the left appears to be a wood closet. However, at the back of the closet there is a door leading to a secret stairway. The narrow staircase winds around the rough brick of the chimney to a room on the third floor.

There have been many theories as to why the stairs were installed. The most probable is that when the second John Turner remodeled the house

House of Seven Gables: 54 Turner Street, Salem, Massachusetts. Open to the public.

Derby House, Salem Maritime Nat. Hist. Site: Derby Street, Salem, Massachusetts. Open to the public.

Peirce-Nichols House: 80 Federal Street, Salem, Massachusetts. Open to the public. Color illustration, p. 27.

Above: Derby House, preserved as a national historic site, became part of the first American estate to be valued at more than a million dollars. The house is furnished with period pieces of Queene Anne and Chippendale designs. Below: The House of Seven Gables, blackened over the years by the salt air, recalls the dreary 17th-century witchcraft trials.

in 1692 he had the hideaway built. That was the time of the original witch hunt in Salem, and since Turner had two young daughters, he possibly wanted a place to hide them should the finger be pointed at them.

The top entrance to the staircase is concealed in the pine-paneling at the side of the fireplace of the room and is opened by pushing a concealed wooden spring in the fireplace.

The Great Chamber on the second floor has recessed windows with comfortable seats. A canopied four-poster bed dominates the room. The parlor, directly below the chamber, contains the desk at which Hawthorne often wrote and the armchair in which he sat during his visits with cousin Susan Ingersoll.

In the 18th century, as the wealth from foreign ports poured into Salem, the homes became more elaborate. One of the best examples of this period is the Derby House, now the oldest brick dwelling in the city. It was built in 1761-1762 by Captain Richard Derby for his son, Elias Hasket Derby.

The house, which faces historic Derby Wharf, is of late Georgian architecture with a gambrel-type roof of slate. Elias Derby (1739-1799), the first American to have an estate valued at $1,000,000, lived in the house for 17 years.

Considerable restoration work has been done on the house, correcting details which had been changed by owners over the years. One was the replacement of the twelve-over-twelve type windows and the duplication of the first paint colors and the earliest example of wallpaper.

The furnishings are those which would be expected in the home of a wealthy merchant. Chippendale and Queen Anne tables, chairs, secretaries and desks. A brass chandelier with an adjustable chain made in Holland about 1750 hangs in the dining room. In the Chippendale secretary of Cuban mahogany are volumes of leather-bound classics brought from England by the Derbys.

In the post-Revolutionary era a more elegant type of residence became popular among the merchant-mariners and one of the finest examples is the Peirce-Nichols House which was built in 1782 for Jerathmiel Peirce. It was designed by Samuel

McIntire and is considered to be one of the finest wooden houses in New England.

Started in 1782, the eastern half was remodeled by McIntire in 1801. Thus, the earlier western portion is Georgian, while the eastern portion is considered Adam or Federal in style.

The front of the house presents an imposing pedimented portico in the Doric style with applied pilasters at the corners and a "captain's walk" on the roof. The front of the house also has a delicate white fence with late 18th-century urns.

The west parlor has a dignified paneled fireplace wall with egg-and-dart and dentil moldings, further embellished with tiles representing Aesop's *Fables*. These are said to have been captured as war booty from the British ship *Brutus*. The room is furnished in the Chippendale style.

The east parlor, "modernized" in 1801, shows the elegance and delicate proportions of the Federal style. Although McIntire never traveled very far from Salem he is known to have collected books and prints from which he became familiar with the English Adam style. He adapted both his spatial proportions and his decorations to the new ideals.

In this style of woodwork he used slim, fluted pilasters, the foliated capital, the rosette, the graceful swag — all replacing the austerity of the strong moldings in his earlier architecture. All the furnishings are authentic in period, and the handsome mahogany blockfront chest-on-chest was made in Massachetts about 1770-1785.

Although the last of the Peirce-Nichols family did not leave the house until 1935, it was bought in 1917 by the Essex Institute of Salem to be preserved along with other historically significant homes in Salem.

Few towns its size have left as many marks in American history as Salem. It was one of the first settlements to become part of the Massachusetts Bay Colony. During the Revolutionary War, it was the only significant American continental port that never fell into British hands. There were the witch trials and the great merchants. Today the many fine homes — such as the House of Seven Gables, Derby House and Peirce-Nichols House — stand as reminders to the richness of that history.

Above: More than 100 years after its construction, John Greenleaf Whittier may have sat and warmed himself before the huge fireplace of his New England homestead, as the wintry winds blowing across Job's Hill inspired the memorable "Snow-Bound."

JOHN GREENLEAF WHITTIER HOMESTEAD

HAVERHILL, MASSACHUSETTS

Home of "Snow-Bound"

The sun that brief December day
Rose cheerless over hills of gray,
And, darkly circled, gave at noon
A sadder light than waning moon.

The opening lines of John Greenleaf Whittier's famous winter idyl, "Snow-Bound," have been familiar to students for well over a century. The word picture of life on a New England farm during a driving storm is a classic of American literature and certainly the best known of Whittier's many poems.

The house which it describes is still standing in Haverhill, Massachusetts, and on a winter's day one can stand on its grounds and imagine the giant drifts and the boys of the family tunneling their way to the barn to feed the animals, and the stories told around the fire as the close-knit family awaited the end of the white fury.

The Whittier Homestead was built by Thomas Whittier in 1688 when he acquired 148 acres of land in a small pleasant valley under the shoulder of Job's Hill. Fernside Brook meanders near the homestead site and provided water for the farm needs and power to turn the mill wheel.

It was here that the poet, a great-great-grandson of Thomas, was born on December 17, 1807. The house is much the same as when Whittier knew it during the years when he was growing up. The large fireplace in the kitchen is easily recognized as the one mentioned in "Snow-Bound." The elevated Mother's Bedroom, built over a rock too large to move, is still to be seen and many of the furnishings, including Whittier's desk, are still in place.

John Greenleaf Whittier Homestead: 305 Whittier Road, Haverhill, Massachusetts. Open to the public.

Outside is the natural stone mounting-block used by generations of children and the doorstone on which the "Barefoot Boy" ate his bowl of milk and bread.

Whittier's family were hard-working New England farm folk ekeing out a living from the land. Whittier lacked the vigorous strength required of farm boys and he soon found he had a natural talent for poetry. This was inspired by the chance visit of Robert Burns, the Scottish poet, to the Whittier home. It was given further impetus by his sister, Mary, who secretly sent one of his first poems to the *Newburyport Free Press*.

The poem was printed and the young editor, William Lloyd Garrison, came in search of the author. Garrison, the famous abolitionist, not only did much to foster Whittier's talent, but also converted him to the cause of the abolition of slavery.

Whittier wrote extensively during his 84 years. The last 56 years he lived in Amesbury, but his thoughts were forever returning to the old Yankee homestead in Haverhill.

Above: The exterior of the Whittier Homestead appears bleak and quiet amid the barren trees and snow of a New England winter. Below: Archibald MacPheadris, a Scot of obscure origin, built this house with his New World fortune.

MACPHEADRIS-WARNER HOUSE

PORTSMOUTH, NEW HAMPSHIRE

House of Two Merchants

Like many of the other famous houses built in New England during the 18th century, the Macpheadris-Warner House at Portsmouth, New Hampshire, was erected by a man who had wide interests in foreign trade and in the development of his region.

Archibald Macpheadris' background remains a mystery. It is not known from where, or when, he immigrated to New Hampshire. There are indications he was of Scots-Irish descent and was perhaps responsible for the influx of people from northern Ireland in the early 18th century.

The Macpheadris-Warner House was built in the latter part of the second decade of the century. There are extant carpenters' bills for interior trim dated 1716, indicating the house was nearing completion at that time. A bill of lading dated May 1716, covers a shipment of furniture from England, and it seems unlikely that the owner would have ordered furniture if he had no place to put it.

Despite his sagacity in business, Macpheadris appears to have made one major mistake in the construction of his home. The house, as first built, had two gables giving the roof in profile the shape of a large "M." It was soon found that the valley between the gables served only to collect the winter snows and cause dampness. As a result the contour of the roof was changed.

The house is considered one of the finest examples of urban brick residences built in America in the first quarter of the 18th century. The design is a familiar one in New England homes of the period; the first floor has two rooms on each side of a central hall, the second floor is similarly laid out. The three principal rooms and the lower and upper halls are completely paneled and in the other rooms the fireplace walls are woodsheathed.

The staircase walls are covered with murals which generally have no relation to each other, either as to subject or to scale. The exceptions are two life-sized portraits separated by a rounded window on the landing. These represent two of five Mohawk Sachems that Colonel Peter Schuyler of Albany took to London in 1710 in an attempt to win that Indian nation's neutrality during the French and Indian War.

In addition to his shipping interest — he owned at least six vessels in 1717 — Macpheadris sought to develop farms in the area surrounding Portsmouth. He also went into partnership with three other men to mine bog iron ore on the Lamprey River and to manufacture iron objects for household and marine use. The enterprise flourished for a time but the ore was of low quality and by 1750 the project was on its last legs.

When Macpheadris died in 1729 he left his share of the iron works to his son, Gilbert, hoping undoubtedly that it would prove the base of a lasting fortune. Gilbert, however, disappeared from the scene about 1735.

The family's only daughter, Mary, was left a childless widow by the death of her husband, John Osborn of Boston. On October 1, 1760, she married Jonathan Warner, described as "a fashionable widower of Portsmouth." Jonathan Warner was born in Portsmouth, the third generation of the family in America. His first marriage was to Mary Nelson of Boston, granddaughter of Lieutenant Governor John Wentworth. After his second marriage to Mrs. Mary (Macpheadris) Osborn on October 1, 1760, he moved into the great brick house where his wife was living, and remained in residence there until his death in 1814. His second wife died in 1780 and he survived a third wife by four years.

Warner was a highly successful merchant sending goods to many parts of the world in his own ships. He became a member of the King's Council in 1766 and the same year was made a justice of the peace, a post he held until his death.

MacPheadris-Warner House: 150 Daniel Street, Portsmouth, New Hampshire. Open to the public.

He ran into trouble with leaders of the Revolutionary movement in August 1776, when he refused to sign the "Association Test" passed by the Continental Congress as an indication of allegiance to the rebellion. As a result he and 14 others were arrested and sent to Exeter. They were released after a short time under bond not to take any action adverse to the colony.

Warner had another run-in with the authorities early in 1777 when the sheriff was ordered by the Committee of Safety to seize a number of hogsheads of rum which the owners had in a warehouse and refused to sell to the Continental Army. Warner had two hogsheads at the warehouse, but the sheriff, after an investigation, ruled that these were no more than the owner might be expected to need for his personal use.

The house also has a lightning rod on the west wall which is said to have been installed under the supervision of Benjamin Franklin during a visit to Portsmouth in 1762.

THE PARSON ASHLEY HOUSE

DEERFIELD, MASSACHUSETTS

The Controversial Parson

The Reverend Jonathan Ashley arrived in Deerfield, Massachusetts, in 1732, fresh from Yale, and for the next 48 years was the center of controversy, theological and political, in the town and a substantial part of the Connecticut Valley.

On his arrival he purchased a house which was to be the Ashley homestead for six generations. Just when the house was built is the subject of much conjecture, but such documents as now exist indicate that it was erected around 1726-1733.

In 1869 Jonathan Ashley, a great-grandson of the Parson, built a new house and the 18th-century parsonage was moved back among the outbuildings to become a tobacco barn and allowed to fall into disrepair. The Yankee farmer descendant of the minister had found that the building was of solid frame. Also, being thrifty, he found this a way to escape the expense of a new barn.

Thus it remained until 1945 — the windows boarded up, clapboards falling away, the roof rotting, the interior nearly stripped of partitions and only a dirt floor where once wide boards had stretched through hallways and the large principal rooms of the first floor.

Fortuitous circumstances combined to rescue the house and led to its restoration and reconstruction. Mr. Frank L. Boyden, Headmaster of Deerfield Academy, purchased the 19th-century Ashley House to provide more dormitory space, but the house was a great distance from the campus. So he conferred with Mr. Henry N. Flynt, chairman of the board of trustees, and a plan was drawn up to move the newer house closer to the academy. Mr. and Mrs. Flynt purchased the land and the original house and brought it back to rejoin the many other colonial homes along the mile-long street.

The task took three years and much of the work was made more difficult because much of the original paneling and bricks and clapboards were beyond reclaim. Working with what was available and following closely the architecture and interior design of houses built about the same period, the task was completed in 1948; and today the house stands much as when the Reverend Ashley knew it when he prepared his lengthy sermons in the study, drank tea in Tory defiance of the Non-Importation Act, and entertained visiting clergymen.

The Reverend Jonathan Ashley was born at Westfield, Massachusetts, November 11, 1712. At the age of 14, accompanied by three first cousins, he left his father's farm, headed for New Haven and the recently established college called Yale. There was a total of 18 students in the class.

He received his degree in 1730 and after a trial

The Parson Ashley House: Deerfield, Massachusetts. Open to the public. Color illustration, pp. 28 - 29.

period was called to Deerfield. The town was already widely known as having been the scene of a bloody raid by the French and Indians in 1704. During his tenure, in the period from 1740 to 1759, the town was to see more attacks in the area by the same forces. Ashley looked on the reprisals by his fellow settlers as Holy Wars to be waged against the French as Papists and the Indians as inventions of Satan.

He preached to the people of Deerfield in the prevailing Calvinistic doctrine; Indian attacks, droughts, crop failures and other misfortunes were to be considered as God's punishment.

At the time of the "Great Awakening," when revivals became popular, he at first agreed with their underlying motive — more conversions. Later, however, he took an opposing stand on the grounds that conversions relying on a deliberate appeal to emotions disregarded the God-given power of reason.

With all his concern for the spiritual welfare of his flock, the Parson, a leading religious figure in Western Massachusetts, also had to concern himself with the welfare of his family. He worked his farm as his neighbors did and he further augmented his meager salary by taking in students preparing for the ministry.

As the winds of rebellion began to sweep the land he made his position known at once — he was a loyal subject of the King. His stand so irritated most of the townspeople that they refused to supply him with firewood, as provided for in his contract.

On another occasion he preached that the Americans who had fallen at Lexington would meet a fearful doom. According to a Deerfield legend, the following week Ashley found his church nailed up.

By 1780 he had so aggravated the townspeople that a move was started to force his dismissal. However, in August of that year he died thus ending the controversy.

Above: A sunflower chest in the Ashley House is a fine example of decorative colonial craftsmanship. Right: The simple furnishings of the kitchen were comfortable in their day but reflect the controversial parson's modest means.

Samuel Chamberlain

Samuel Chamberlain

ADAMS HOUSE
QUINCY, MASSACHUSETTS

Four Generations of Adamses at the "Old House"

It would be impossible to write a history of the United States without including the name of the Adams family of Quincy, Massachusetts. They not only made history from the beginning of the Republic, but they also wrote about it extensively.

Two members of the family, father and son, were the second and sixth Presidents of the United States. A son of the latter was President Lincoln's Minister to the Court of St. James during the Civil War. His four sons distinguished themselves as politicians, diplomats and historians.

The house was named "Peacefield" by John Adams when he purchased the property in September 1787. In later years the family referred to it affectionately as the "Old House."

The original house was built in 1731 by a Major Leonard Vassall, a wealthy West Indian sugar planter, who moved to Massachusetts in 1723. It consisted of a paneled room, west entry and dining room on the ground floor, two bedrooms on the second floor and three smaller rooms in the attic. The kitchen and servants' quarters were not attached to the house.

John Adams was still Minister to Great Britain when he bought the house from Leonard Vassall Borland, a grandson of the builder. Adams and his independent-minded wife, Abigail, took possession the following year on his return from England.

While he was serving as President he added a large gabled ell containing the long room, the east entry and an upstairs study. In 1836 his son built the passage along the north side of the house connecting the two ells. Thirty-three years later Charles Francis Adams added 30 feet to the kitchen ell for servants' quarters, and the following year he had a stone library built overlooking his grandmother's garden. Years later the stone stable was built.

John Adams lived at the house the year around from the time of his retirement from the Presidency in 1801 until his death July 4, 1826, the same day Thomas Jefferson died. It was used as a summer home by both John Quincy Adams and Charles Francis Adams. A good deal of the furniture reflects the diplomatic history of the family, having been brought from many parts of Europe.

John Adams, a forthright if somewhat irascible man, became active in the American Revolutionary movement from the outset. His role in opposing the Stamp Act did not deter him several years later from showing his moral courage by defending the British Captain, Thomas Preston, who was charged with murder in the Boston "Massacre."

He was a delegate to the First and Second Continental Congresses and was one of the framers of the Declaration of Independence. At the close of the war he began his diplomatic career, first in France and later in Holland and in England. He served as Washington's Vice-President and was elected to the Presidency in 1796.

John Quincy Adams, born July 11, 1767, traveled extensively with his father in Europe, but returned to the United States to attend Harvard College. His acute intelligence was apparent at an early age, and John Quincy began his diplomatic career under Washington as Minister to the Netherlands (1794) and later was his father's Minister to Prussia. He also served as the American envoy to England and in 1817 became President Monroe's Secretary of State.

In 1825 he took the oath of office as sixth President of the United States. He retired to Quincy in 1829 with the idea of writing history, but two years later he was elected to Congress and served for 17 years.

Charles Francis Adams, son of the sixth President, was born August 18, 1807, and spent much of

---

Adams National Historic Site: 135 Adams Street, Quincy, Massachusetts. Open to the public.

Above: The Adams' mansion, preserved as a national historic site, was the home of two Presidents and a long line of scholars and statesmen. Below: Much of the history made by this prominent family was later recorded in the upstairs study.

his boyhood in Europe, but dutifully returned to attend Harvard. Unlike his father and grandfather, Charles was an even-tempered man and he served in the Massachusetts Legislature and in 1858 was elected to Congress. In 1861, following a family tradition, he went to the Court of St. James as American Minister and served there during the trying years of the Civil War. On his retirement in 1868 he refused to take the presidency of Harvard and retired to the Old House.

He wrote on history for the *North American Review*, published the letters of his grandmother Abigail Adams and *The Works of John Adams* in 10 volumes; he also published a biography of his grandfather and the memoirs of his father.

Four sons moved onto the scene of history in the mid-19th century. John Quincy, born in 1833, was prominent in Massachusetts politics and served on the staff of Governor Andrews during the Civil War. His brother, Charles Francis, Jr., born two years later, commanded a Negro regiment in the Civil War — the first unit to enter Richmond after Lee evacuated the city.

The third son, Henry Adams, studied civil law in Berlin after his graduation from Harvard. He traveled around the world for many years and became his father's secretary in London during the latter's diplomatic mission. In 1868 he took a post teaching history at Harvard and edited the *North American Review*. He wrote several biographies, two novels, a nine-volume history of the United States, *Mont Saint Michel and Chartres*, and the American classic, *The Education of Henry Adams*.

Brooks Adams, the youngest son, was the last of the family to occupy the Old House. He was also a Harvardian and served as his father's secretary during the Alabama Claims Arbitration. His works included *The Emancipation of Massachusetts*, *Law of Civilization and Decay*, *America's Economic Supremacy*, and *Theory of Social Revolution*.

The family still remains on the scene in the modern age. A Charles Francis Adams developed one of the leading electronics firms of the nation during the past generation. But today the Old House is the Adams National Historic Site, as it seemed destined to become as one distinguished generation of Adamses followed another.

OLD MANSE

CONCORD, MASSACHUSETTS

The House of Emerson and Hawthorne

The Reverend William Emerson stood in the field between his home and action at the Old North Bridge on the morning of April 19, 1775, and watched the firing of "the shot heard round the world."

His wife and five children watched the first battle of the American Revolution from the upstairs windows of the manse, little dreaming that the young minister himself would march off to war as a chaplain and be dead within a year, a victim of camp fever near Rutland, Vermont.

It was the minister's grandson, Ralph Waldo Emerson, poet, philosopher, essayist, who immortalized the stand of the Minutemen with his Concord Hymn, written in 1837:

By the rude bridge that arched the flood,
Their flag to April's breeze unfurled,
Here once the embattled farmers stood
And fired the shot heard round the world.

The sage of the New England Transcendentalists spent part of his boyhood in the house. Four years after his grandfather's death in 1776, the widow married the Reverend Ezra Ripley who had succeeded to the pastorate. Ralph Waldo's father, also William, was brought up in the Old Manse.

The most famous occupant of the house, however, was Nathaniel Hawthorne who brought his bride to the Old Manse on July 9, 1842, for a four-

Old Manse: Monument Street, Concord, Massachusetts. Open to the public.

NEW ENGLAND HOUSES

*Above: The imposing façade of the Peirce-Nichols
House in Salem, Massachusetts, displays a pedimented
Doric-style portico, a "captain's walk" on the roof and a
delicate fence with 18th-century urns reflecting the
tastes of merchant-builder Jerathmiel Peirce.*

Above: Cherubs float on the blue ceiling of the rococo library at Marble House, former home of the William Vanderbilts in Newport, Rhode Island. The shelves and paneling are of English walnut carved with the swirling shapes characteristic of the ornate style.

Above: The 18th-century home of Parson Jonathan Ashley as it is today, fully restored. In 1869 his great-grandson built a new house, moving the original structure to a back lot where it remained relegated to the status of a tobacco barn for over 70 years.

29

Above: The grand home built by merchant John Brown in Providence, Rhode Island, set architectural precedents for future houses, as in the slight projection crowned by a pediment in the center of the façade of the three-story brick mansion.

Left: The mahogany secretary (c. 1760) found in the morning room of the John Brown House in Providence is the only known piece on which there are nine carved shells. To the left is a self-portrait of American artist Robert Feke; on the right, his wife Eleanor Cozzens.

(Continued from page 26)

year stay. Hawthorne rented the house from the Ripley family which had possession from 1780 until 1939 when it was turned over to the Trustees of Reservations.

The house was built in 1769 and remains today essentially the same as when the Reverend William Emerson moved into it. A dormer and a bay window were added in 1880 by the Reverend Samuel Ripley.

The Old Manse is set back from the road and Hawthorne noted: "Certainly it had little in common with those ordinary abodes which stand so imminent upon the road that every passer-by can thrust his head . . . into the domestic circle."

It is a two-and-a-half story clapboard structure with a gambrel roof and has two pedimented doorways. For its day it was a large house. There are four rooms and a central hall downstairs, in addition to the usual sheds in the rear. On the second floor there are four bedrooms and the third floor has several small chambers for visitors. One room on the third floor is known as the "saints chamber." It was kept for the use of traveling clergymen. Over the fireplace Ralph Waldo Emerson's father wrote at the age of eleven, "Began Greek, Jan. 26, 1780."

Hawthorne had a reputation as a "loner," but it is apparent from his diaries that the happiest years of his life were spent at the Old Manse. Henry Thoreau, Dr. Ellery Channing and Emerson were among his visitors.

The garden and the orchard were a delight to him; perhaps his interest in them stemmed from his experience at Brook Farm, a communal project.

His wife, Sophia Peabody Hawthorne, did much to banish the gloom from the house. She took down the dreary pictures of old ministers from the walls, painted the chairs white with flower adornment, and brightened up the surroundings while her husband worked on *Mosses from an Old Manse.*

The Hawthornes left their mark on the house. On one window pane one can still see, scratched with Mrs. Hawthorne's diamond, a note about her daughter:

Una Hawthorne stood on this window sill January 22, 1845, while the trees were all glass chandeliers, a goodly show, which she liked much tho' only ten months old.

Below: Appearing a little sorrowful during the transition of seasons, the Old Manse was witness to "the shot heard round the world" and later provided shelter for the imaginative spirits of Ralph Waldo Emerson and Nathaniel Hawthorne.

JOHN BROWN HOUSE

PROVIDENCE, RHODE ISLAND

A Place of New Departures

The John Brown House in Providence, Rhode Island, was built by John, third of the famous "Four Brown Brothers" — Nicholas, Joseph, John and Moses — leading 18th-century merchants in Rhode Island.

The house, now headquarters of The Rhode Island Historical Society, was designed by Joseph Brown, a professor of natural philosophy at Rhode Island College, now Brown University. He died before work was started in 1786.

The brick mansion standing on a hill has three stories and an attic. Like many of its contemporaries it has four rooms on each floor divided by a wide central hall running north and south. The ends of the heavy oak beams sustaining the floors are embedded in the massive exterior walls. Even the interior partitions are made of solid brick.

In designing the house Joseph Brown incorporated several new features which were later included in other homes in the Providence area. One of these was the inclusion of four chimneys rather than the customary two. He also made provision for a slight projection, crowned by a pediment in the center of the façade and a Palladian window over the entrance.

The rooms of the first and second floors contain fine furniture which is of Rhode Island origin. Portraits, silverware and other decorative objects have been chosen, in as far as possible, for their close association with Rhode Island and the period during which John Brown lived in the house.

An ell and the third floor of the house contain collections of historical relics. Brown's chariot, built in 1782 and believed to be the oldest existing American-built vehicle, is in the Coach House.

A heavy cornice and deep frieze with carving in relief decorates the central hallway. The builder used mahogany for baseboards, window seats, chair rails, doors and the dominating staircase with its twisted balusters and ramped rail.

The dining room is presently decorated with modern scenic wallpaper depicting the first inauguration of President Washington (1789) at New York City. Miss Nancy McClelland, who designed the paper, chose the theme because of the strong friendship between Washington and John Brown.

The wallpaper, however, is not the only tribute to Washington that is part of the John Brown House tradition. In 1790, he was reportedly the guest of Brown, and the latter named several ships after Washington, as well as the bridge he built from Providence to East Providence. In addition to Washington, John Quincy Adams, too, was an admirer of the Brown House, writing in 1789: "We only saw the outside of it, which is the most magnificent and elegant private mansion I have ever seen on this continent."

Brown took part in one of the first actions of the American Revolution, leading a group of Providence men who burned the British revenue schooner *Gaspee* to the waterline after she had run aground in Narragansett Bay on June 10, 1772, while pursuing a suspected contraband runner.

He was chosen a Rhode Island delegate to the Continental Congress in 1784 and again in the following year, but he did not take his seat. He led the successful fight to overcome Rhode Island's opposition to the adoption of the Constitution and served in Congress, 1799-1801.

With his son-in-law, John Francis, he formed the firm of Brown and Francis in 1787 and was very successful in trade with the East Indies and China. Along with his brothers he contributed heavily to what is now Brown University and was treasurer of that institution for 20 years.

John Brown House: 52 Power Street, Providence, Rhode Island. Open to the public. Color illustration, p. 30.

Eugene Mitchell

Above: The Shaker Stone Barn's unique design is the result of religious tenets emphasizing functional requirements. Right: A chest and stove, with Shaker innovations, have clean, simple lines which also reflect Millennial Laws.

HANCOCK SHAKER VILLAGE
PITTSFIELD, MASSACHUSETTS

The Shaker Legacy

The Hancock Shaker Village of today, permanently etched in the landscape and heritage of the Massachusetts Berkshires, is only a vestige of the resourceful and industrious community which thrived in the years prior to the Civil War. An offshoot of the first Shaker village at Niskayuna, New York, the community at Hancock was firmly established in 1790, after a visit by "Mother Ann" (Ann Lee), founder of the sect.

An illiterate, English immigrant, she brought with her to this country a curious combination of Quaker and French-Calvinistic beliefs which emphasized celibacy, thrift, industry and good morals. The actual name of the sect was the United Society of Believers in Christ's Second Appearing, but because of the fact that many of the members would

shake and tremble at prayer meetings, outsiders began to call them "Shaking Quakers." The term "Shakers," originally one of derision, was eventually adopted by the group itself in common usage.

Directed in religious and secular affairs alike by the Millennial Laws, a Shaker-produced document which established Mother Ann as the embodiment of Christ in a woman, this religious people abhorred the aesthetic value of beauty, calling it a device of the devil. Nonetheless, and perhaps because of this, they proved to be one of the most inventive single groups in America.

The circular Stone Barn at the Hancock Village is characteristic of the restraint and practicality with which the Shakers applied their religious beliefs. Achieving a circumference of 270 feet, this

Hancock Shaker Village: U.S. Route 20, Pittsfield, Massachusetts. Open to the public.

building was designed to facilitate the housing and tending of 52 head of cattle on the ground floor, while hay wagons could be simultaneously driven around the second-story loft and unloaded. Making functional use of the surrounding terrain, the Shakers constructed the building so that each of its two major levels opened onto a corresponding level of ground. Above the second level is a louvered cupola, designed to provide ventilation and ease the danger of spontaneous fires in the hay. From the interior of this cupola an elaborate framework extends throughout the building; however, its appearance was derived solely from its functional purpose.

The remainder of the 16 buildings at Hancock include a conventional barn, dormitory where men and women slept separately, meeting house and a variety of shops and utility quarters; and like the Stone Barn, they were designed and constructed with austere simplicity. An expansive garden, partially restored and replanted now, covered many acres at one time.

Typical of the absence of adornment inside the Shaker buildings is the dining hall, where the men and women ate at separate tables. Except for a peg board, on which chairs were hung after meals to facilitate cleaning, the walls are barren. Furniture made by Shakers also offered no luxury, being constructed only to fulfill its utilitarian purposes. Nonetheless, Shaker furniture, especially the slat-back rocking chairs and side chairs, was bought by many outsiders during the first half of the 19th century, primarily because it was cheap and well made. This furniture is much admired today because its clean, pure lines appeal to modern tastes.

The Shakers' emphasis on the utilitarian purposes of things stimulated an unusual capacity for invention. For whatever ceased to be of greatest functional value was discarded as soon as a replacement could be found. In this quest for a simpler, more effective means to accomplish daily tasks, they are credited with the invention of the circular saw, clothespin, flatbroom, a cheese-making device, apple peeler and slicer, a machine for weaving straw bonnets and a box stove which approached modern central heating in its efficiency.

Today there are only two active Shaker communities remaining in the United States: Canterbury, New Hampshire, and Sabbathday Lake, Maine. When the village at Hancock diminished to only two members in 1960, it was offered for public sale. Convinced that this intriguing segment of American heritage should not be erased from the national memory, a group of local citizens acquired the property, dedicating a permanent memorial to the Shaker movement throughout the United States.

Below: A woodcut of Hancock Shaker Village, rendered by John Warner in 1841, accurately portrays the lack of adornment in the Shaker way of life. Their deep concern for functional standards produced many of the useful Shaker inventions.

HARRISON GRAY OTIS HOUSE

BOSTON, MASSACHUSETTS

Bulfinch's Boston Brick

Boston's old West End has largely disappeared. On the northern fringe modern high-rise apartment buildings line the Charles River and to the south the towering structures of the new Government Center have brought a mid-20th-century look to one of the oldest sections of the city.

In the midst of all this rush to modernity stands the Harrison Gray Otis House, completed in 1797 for one of the city's most prominent political and social figures. Harrison Gray Otis, a nephew of the Revolutionary War hero, James Otis, was a leader of the Federalist party in Congress, and is said to have had the oratorical powers of his illustrious uncle.

He was a lawyer-statesman, member of the U.S. House of Representatives and the Senate. He also served as Mayor of Boston.

The house which bears his name is considered an outstanding example of Federal architecture and is believed to have been the work of Charles Bulfinch, designer of the Massachusetts State House.

Otis stayed in the house only five years and then built another on Mount Vernon Street on the slope of Beacon Hill. Since 1916 the house has been the headquarters of the Society for the Preservation of New England Antiquities.

At the rear of the house, the society maintains an architectural museum, the only one of its kind outside of Russia. On display here are building

Harrison Gray Otis House: 141 Cambridge Street, Boston, Massachusetts. Open to the public.

Below: The dining room of the Harrison Gray Otis House, the original woodwork and plaster moldings still intact, reflects the elegance of the Federal style and period. Original Sheraton and Hepplewhite designs were used in the restoration.

Richard Merrill

accessories such as doors, cornices, balustrades, etc., some of which have survived over 300 years. Included in the collection is one of the capitals from the Old State House in Boston.

The front doorway with its delicate fanlight and eight-panel door, the plaster cornice and frieze and the beautiful staircase have all survived the ravages of time virtually intact.

In recent years most of the high-ceilinged interior has been carefully restored and furnished. Sheraton and Hepplewhite furniture of the period has been returned to the front parlor and the arrangement of window hangings is based on a curtain shown in a painting by Ralph Earl dated 1796. The fabric of the draperies and upholstery is a reproduction of a late 18th-century silk damask.

The dining room still has its original woodwork and the classic motifs in molded plaster have been painted green with the details picked out in cream color, following evidence discovered under many coats of paint. The period furniture includes a set of 12 Sheraton mahogany side chairs with leather seats, circa 1800, which belonged to Mary Otis, half sister of Harrison Gray Otis.

Imitation damask wallpapers and borders in the withdrawing room are careful reproductions of the originals that were found under layers of wallpaper. "Captain Cook" and "Paysage Indien" wallpapers hang in the chamber above the parlor.

During the 19th century the house underwent many vicissitudes as ownership kept changing hands. At one time it was a rooming house and there are records to show that during its long career it was also a ladies' Turkish bath. Today it is one of the few brick houses of its period that remains in Boston, its eight restored rooms firmly a part of a proud city's heritage.

Below: The Harrison Gray Otis House is preserved in one of the oldest sections of Boston. A sketch discovered in the papers of Harrison Gray Otis has led to the belief that architect Charles Bulfinch designed the house.

Samuel Chamberlain

Above. The 22-room Gore mansion, constructed of pink brick laid in Flemish bond, was built after a fire destroyed Christopher Gore's summer residence while he was in England in 1799. It was designed by French architect Jaques Guillaume Legrand.

GORE PLACE

WALTHAM, MASSACHUSETTS

Waltham's Palatial "Farm"

Christopher Gore, seventh governor of Massachusetts, described his home in Waltham as "my farm."

Actually the magnificent estate, eight miles west of Boston, is one of the finest examples of Federal architecture of the early 19th century. Its setting on a rise, with rolling lawns stretching southward to the Charles River, gives it the appearance of an English gentleman's manor.

The stately three-storied building was the scene of many official functions in the days when Gore was Governor of Massachusetts (1809-1810) and later from 1813 to 1816 when he served in the United States Senate.

The 22-room mansion was planned by the Gores while they were in England. Mr. Gore, after serving as the first U.S. Attorney for Massachusetts, was sent to London in 1796 as chief commissioner under the Jay Treaty to settle claims in England.

In 1799 he was informed that the summer residence he had in Waltham had been destroyed by fire and he and Mrs. Gore immediately set about planning its replacement on the 48-acre property.

This holding was gradually expanded to 400 acres, but today the historic park on which the Gore Place stands is 76 acres.

There has always been a question about the architect, but the Gores referred quite frequently in their letters from Paris to a Jacques Guillaume Legrand, whose work had a great influence on Federal architecture. In any case, the plans were made overseas and construction was started shortly after the Gores returned to the United States in 1804.

The exterior design has a finely proportioned central block flanked by two lower wings with pedimented pavilions on either end. The walls of the house are of the smallest of pink brick laid in Flemish bond. A sandstone terrace was designed to accommodate horsemen as well as coaches.

On entering the mansion from the north, palatial marble floors lead to the two-story State Reception Hall, which has a semi-elliptical interior wall with curved doors and thresholds. Two fireplaces flank the wall and above them hang the portraits of Governor and Mrs. Gore.

Gore Place: 52 Gore Street, Waltham, Massachusetts. Open to the public.

One of the outstanding features of this elegant room is the flying staircase which circles upwards with no visible means of support. Beyond the Reception Hall is the oval dining room, facing south, which is also two stories high. Above is the governor's oval study and a bedroom.

The two wings contain intimate living quarters on the first level and on the mezzanine. The west wing contains an herb room in which the governor and his wife took great interest. The east wing mezzanine has a nursery, although the Gores had no children but many nieces and nephews.

The huge English billiard room, just off the main entrance, was an incentive for many young Harvardians to make the walk from Cambridge to Waltham on Sunday afternoons.

In his time the governor did work the land and his place was known as one of the best farms in the area. The formal gardens, attributed to Humphrey Repton, the English landscape gardener, complete the natural setting for the governor's manor.

Above: The flying staircase which circles upward without visible means of support in the two-story reception room of Gore Place is one of the outstanding features of this Federal-style mansion. Below: A sideboard in the oval dining room is among the original furnishings which have been retained from the possessions of the seventh governor of Massachusetts.

THE STARBUCK HOUSES
NANTUCKET, MASSACHUSETTS

The Three Bricks

From the time Nantucket was first settled in the middle of the 17th century, men of that small island off the southeastern coast of Massachusetts have been going down to the sea in ships.

During the first half of the 19th century it became the most important whaling port in the world. Ships from Nantucket searched far and wide across the Pacific Ocean for the giant mammals and the whale oil that lit the lamps in the business establishments and homes along the East Coast and even in Europe.

Twenty-three ships, three schooners and three sloops at one time or another during the period flew the blue-and-white house flag of Joseph Starbuck and Sons. Near the end of his career Starbuck figured that his six "favorite" ships had made over 50 voyages and brought back 80,000 barrels of oil that marketed for an estimated $2,500,000.

One of these was the 384-ton *Three Brothers* which was launched in 1833 and in seven voyages brought back 16,000 barrels of oil with an estimated value of $480,000. The *Three Brothers* was especially dear to Joseph Starbuck because it was named for his three sons, all of whom worked with him in the marketing of the oil and the outfitting and building of the ships that went looking for it.

Joseph was the son of Thomas Starbuck who had built the family fortune in the 18th century. Joseph's brothers, Rueben, Simeon, Levi and Judah had all chosen whaling; Judah was lost at sea. Joseph Starbuck preferred to remain at home and handle the accounts for his father. He eventually took over the business and his three sons, George, Matthew and William, soon found their place along with their father in the family firm.

The elder Starbuck showed his independence of mind in many ways: First by being married to Sally Gardner in 1797 before a Justice of the Peace, an action frowned on by his Quaker parents, and second, in his ideas about home construction.

His first venture in home building came about 1807 when he built a house on the highest section of the New Dollar Lane land, near the head of Main Street. Not content with following the simple architecture favored by the Quakers, who preferred a lean-to house built around a chimney, Joseph decided his home would have two stories front and back. In addition he had two chimneys so placed that there would be fireplaces in each of the eight rooms. In any room a person could stand back to the fireplace and look out windows at the side and front. The town also expressed shock when he included a central hall on both floors and added a basement with a fireplace for cooking.

It was in this house that his three sons and four daughters were born. The daughters grew up and all married successfully, as they say. The three sons were taking a lively interest in the ever expanding business and Joseph Starbuck began to think of a new project.

Always interested in the development of the town of Nantucket he began to look around to see where other families of substance were locating and he chose Main Street. There he would build three brick houses, one for each of his sons.

He had many discussions about the project with William Hadwen, a Newport silversmith who had moved to the island and married Eunice Starbuck. The son-in-law had very definite ideas of what would be new and fashionable and he was not bashful about telling his wife's father about his ideas.

Hadwen argued that the houses being planned were not new in design, but the same wooden houses "covered with bricks." The silversmith was at the same time planning to build two brick mansions across the street from the Starbuck site. He

The Starbuck Houses: Main Street, Nantucket, Massachusetts. Private residences.

prevailed on his father-in-law to incorporate some of his ideas for the entrances while keeping the bricks and the general plan of the houses.

Starbuck was finally talked into adding two pillars with Ionic capitals to a projecting entrance. He also agreed to abandon the famed Nantucket design of having stairs come up from either side to a platform, and place the steps straight up from the sidewalk. Hadwen then suggested modern windows for the front of the house and a balustrade on the eaves of the roof.

Work was started on the "Three Bricks" early in 1837 and when they were completed about two years later Joseph was more than satisfied with the results.

A wide-paneled front door led to a high-ceilinged hall and the foot of the staircase winding to the second floor. Double parlors were at the right of the hall and on the left was a "front setting-room" and behind it a dining room. There was no door between the dining room and the kitchen, and food and dishes were passed through an opening in the wall.

Each room had a fireplace or grate which fed into end chimneys. The standard "captain's walk"

was eliminated in favor of a cupola with cut corners in the center of each roof. The front edge of the roof was decorated with a white balustrade, with panels interrupting the line of balusters.

On the opposite side of the street, William Hadwen built his two portico houses each with four giant white columns under a pediment. The houses were set back from the street.

When the "Three Bricks" were finished the three brothers and their families moved in, George occupied the "West Brick," Matthew the "Middle Brick" and William the "East Brick."

Today Nantucket is "quaint," the hustle and bustle of the whaling days having disappeared over a century ago. And Joseph Starbuck was one of the first to realize the end was coming when his agent in Boston, Josiah Bradlee, wrote to him in 1855 with the information that two chemists in the area had developed kerosene. The need for sending men and ships 10,000 miles on two- and three-year voyages was near its end. But Joseph Starbuck had accomplished what he had set out to do — build the three most elegant homes on Nantucket.

Below: A stubborn man, Joseph Starbuck defied Quaker architectural traditions in the design of his own house, but in the three houses for his sons it was with great reluctance that he included innovations of pillars and balustraded roofs.

MARBLE HOUSE
NEWPORT, RHODE ISLAND

The Age of Ostentation

Bellevue Avenue in Newport, Rhode Island, was shrouded by fog the night of August 19, 1892, when suddenly all the lights of Marble House, both gas and electric, were turned on and one of the great spectacles in the history of Newport began. Mr. and Mrs. William K. Vanderbilt had opened their sumptuous new mansion to their friends for the first time, and the visitors were overwhelmed. It was soon acknowledged to be one of the finest houses to be built during this period, sometimes called the American Renaissance.

Richard Morris Hunt — who had designed The Breakers for Mr. Vanderbilt's brother Cornelius, the famous financier — designed Marble House in the fashion of Louis XIV, who was greatly admired by both Mr. and Mrs. Vanderbilt. Some say that the White House played a part in Hunt's inspiration, while others mention the Petit Trianon at Versailles. In any case it is lavish throughout, in a summer resort noted for its lavish homes, many of which were built after Marble House.

The entrance hall to the mansion is 20 feet high and is lined and paved with yellow marble from the Monte Arenti quarry near Montagnola, Italy. The ceiling has stucco relief in the form of masks and elaborate arabesques, i.e., ornamental fruit, foliage and animals.

Two Gobelin tapestries in gold frames hang to the right and left of the entrance hall. Beneath the tapestries is a large table on one side and a low cabinet of 19th-century buhlwork with an ebony frame and brass and tortoise-shell inlay. A splendid grille of soft steel, with a gun-metal finish and gilt bronze, screens the entrance. Four posts in the shape of Corinthian pilasters, divide the grille into three bays, the central one forming the door.

The richest of the rooms is the Gold Room, which served as a ballroom at some of the extravagant receptions and dances held by the Vanderbilts.

The outstanding ornamentation in the room is found in the gilt-wood panels in carved relief, believed to be the work of Karl Bitter, a protégé of architect Hunt. All the panels are done in red, green and yellow gold.

The Allard mantelpiece consists of bronze figures set on Fleur de Pêche marble. Old Age and Youth hold candelabras and between them is the mask of Dionysius or Bacchus, the god of wine, with garlands of ormolu flowers. Everything about the room speaks of opulence and grandeur.

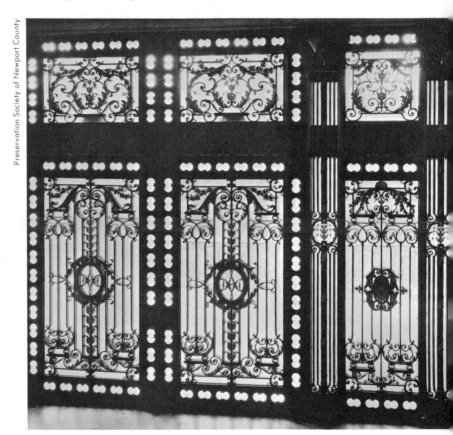

Above: Many ornate features incorporated into the design of William K. Vanderbilt's Marble House are adaptations from the Palaces of the Grand and the Petit Trianon at Versailles. Wrought-iron grating was copied from the French style.

Marble House: Bellevue Avenue, Newport, Rhode Island. Open to the public. Color illustration, p. 28.

Preservation Society of Newport County

The Gothic Room is a sober contrast. The room was designed to house a valuable collection of Gothic miniatures, crucifixes and small art objects, on display in glass cases.

The terrace hall opens onto a marble court between the wings occupied by the library and the Gothic Room. Here again yellow Siena marble is the dominating theme on floors and walls. The library was designed in the rococo style of the 18th century. The closed bookshelves and paneling are of English walnut and are carved with swirling shapes of the style.

Ostentatious decoration is to be found throughout the entire first floor of the mansion and reaches even to the bedrooms on the second floor.

In 1895 the house was the scene of a magnificent party honoring the debut of Consuelo Vanderbilt, who later became the Duchess of Marlborough. A year later the Vanderbilts were divorced and Mrs. Vanderbilt married O.H.P. Belmont. After his death in 1908, she returned to Marble House which had been closed for 12 years and that summer gave a garden party to which the public was invited. It was to promote the cause of woman suffrage.

In 1932 the house was sold to Frederick H. Prince of Boston, and it remained in his family until 1963 when it was bought from his trust by the Preservation Society of Newport County.

Below: The Gothic Room marks an abrupt departure from the 17th- and 18th-century French style which is dominant throughout the rest of Marble House. Mantelpiece was imported from Italy where sculptors modeled Gothic figures in plaster.

Above: Combining both Greek and French designs, Marble House was named for the wide variety of marble used in its construction. During the American Renaissance of architecture, it was considered among the finest homes in the country.

II
MIDDLE ATLANTIC
HOUSES

PENNSBURY MANOR
MORRISVILLE, PENNSYLVANIA

William Penn's Manor

William Penn came to America with perhaps the most idealistic plans of any of those who left the religiously distraught shores of Europe. He was seeking a place not only for the members of the Society of Friends but for any and all who were non-conformists in England, France, Holland, Germany and Ireland.

According to tradition, he was able to obtain the grant of land through an agreement with King Charles II, who owed his father, Vice-Admiral Sir William Penn, the sum of 16,000 pounds sterling for services rendered. The King was more than ready to settle the debt for unknown wilderness across the ocean.

Penn was not always the calm, pacifist Quaker of his later years. He engaged in riots while at Oxford, and while briefly in charge of his father's estates in Ireland he had led armed raids against those who would oppose the rules of the estate.

He settled the claim with the King in 1681 and the following year traveled to his new land with all the rights of a feudal lord. However, Penn sought to make the new land a refuge for all people. His ideals were not always followed by those around him, but he never deviated from his purpose.

In 1683 the site for Penn's home in the New World was chosen. It was located on the Delaware River, in Lower Bucks County, about 25 miles north of Philadelphia. As might be expected, he planned the house, the surrounding buildings and the gardens after the fashion of the English and Irish manor houses to which he was accustomed. Many of the original materials were brought from England, but the bricks and timbers are believed to have been shaped locally.

While the house was still under construction Penn had to return to England and he left the rest of the construction to his manager, James Harrison. The original manor house indicates that Penn had a love of wide spaciousness in his home and in the gardens surrounding it.

The extent of the rooms, the wide doorways and the broad casement windows looking out on the countryside indicate a man who loved the gardens, fields and woods. The great hall was large enough to accommodate groups of visitors on all occasions.

The easiest approach to the house was by the Delaware River and, from the landing, a promenade

Pennsbury Manor: U. S. Route 1, Morrisville, Pennsylvania. Open to the public.

Above: The rear of Pennsbury Manor, headquarters for William Penn's Society of Friends, is flanked by the bake-and-brew house. Below: Interior displays crude implements of the settlers and medicinal herbs hanging from exposed beams.

lined with poplars mounted over a succession of terraces to the front door of the mansion — the home of America's most prominent Quaker.

William Markham, Penn's cousin and deputy governor of the colony, chose the site for Pennsbury weeks before Penn arrived in America. On July 25, 1682, Penn sat down with a group of Indian Sachems and signed a treaty. The signing has been depicted in Benjamin West's painting, done 93 years after the event, showing the Quaker Penn and his neighbors-to-be making the arrangement.

In the contract Penn agreed to pay 350 fathoms of wampum (about one-half mile), 300 gilders, 20 white blankets, 20 fathoms of "strawd waters," 60 fathoms of coarse woolen fabric (or duffields), 20 coats, 40 shirts, 20 kettles, 20 guns, pipes, scissors, shoes, combs, hoes, tobacco, knives, two *anchers* (an ancher is about ten gallons) of rum, cider and beer.

Penn had hoped to make the manor his home for the rest of his life, but political and personal affairs in London forced him to return in 1684 and he did not see the manor again until 1699. By that time his first wife had died and it was his second wife, Hannah, who accompanied him with a daughter of his first marriage, Letitia. During his years in England the Protestant Revolution placed William and Mary in power and the once favorite of the Stuarts found himself suspected of treason. It was not until 1693 that he was cleared

Penn returned in the fall of 1699 and with his wife and grown daughter took up residence in Philadelphia until Pennsbury Manor could be put in order. They spent the following year there, along with John, the only one of Penn's children born in America.

In 1701 London threatened to make Pennsylvania a Crown Colony and Penn insisted on going back to fight the idea. His wife refused to stay in America and returned with him. It was the last time he saw the New World.

The Penns owned this land until about the time of the Revolutionary War. After the Penns departed the manor fell into semi-ruin. In the early 1930's a group met and set up plans to restore the famed homestead of the founder of the state. Through their efforts and those of others the stately mansion now stands again on the shores of the Delaware a fitting tribute to that idealistic man, William Penn.

VAN CORTLANDT MANOR
TARRYTOWN, NEW YORK
SUNNYSIDE
CROTON-ON-THE-HUDSON, NEW YORK

Life and Literature in the Hudson River Valley

The Hudson River Valley is one of the most scenic regions of the nation and, since the days when the Dutch first settled the area, it has been the location of many famous homes. Two of the most famous are Van Cortlandt Manor, at the confluence of the Hudson and Croton Rivers, and Washington Irving's home, Sunnyside, some 12 miles south.

Oloff Van Cortlandt was the first of the family to reach New Amsterdam. He arrived in 1638 as a soldier for the Dutch West India Company. Within a few years he left the company and went into business for himself. He was highly successful as a merchant, brewer and politician. He was one of the Dutch burghers prominent in the negotiations which led to the surrender of New Amsterdam to the English in 1664 and later was an alderman and deputy Mayor of New York.

His oldest son, Stephanus Van Cortlandt, entered business at an early age and, like his father, pursued parallel careers in business and public service. He served as a member of the council of Sir Edmond Andros, the English Governor, and in

Van Cortlandt Manor: Croton-on-Hudson, New York. Open to the public.
Sunnyside: West Sunnyside Lane, Tarrytown, New York. Open to the public. Color illustration, p. 50.

MIDDLE ATLANTIC HOUSES

*Above: Wheatland, the stately home of bachelor
President James Buchanan in Lancaster, Pennsylvania,
is reminiscent of coaches, crinolines and the gracious living of the 19th century. The mansion is set on a gentle
slope with spacious lawns and a tree-lined drive.*

*Above: The magnificent Red Room in the White
House depicts an early 19th-century Empire parlor.
Walls are hung in cerise silk with gold scroll borders and
a gilt wooden chandelier with Classic Revival ornament
complements fine examples of French and American furniture.*

Right: The White House collection contains many fine paintings representative of some of the country's leading artists. Among them is Howard Chandler Christy's charming portrait of the gracious and popular Grace Goodhue Coolidge found in the China Room.

Below: The Blue Room's elegant oval form, with three windows facing the south grounds of the White House, is matched by its fashionable furnishings. It was redecorated in 1962 in a style which enhances the Bellangé chairs acquired by President Monroe.

Above: Sunnyside, Washington Irving's
picturesque 19th-century home on the Hudson
River in Tarrytown, New York, reflects the whimsy and
romanticism of the renowned author whose graceful
prose gave readers the delightful Ichabod Crane.

Above: John Wesley Jarvis' portrayal of Washington Irving captures the imaginative spirit of this lawyer, statesman and literary figure. At his sequestered Sunnyside in Tarrytown, New York, he enjoyed the distinction of being the first man of American letters.

(Continued from page 46)

1677, at the age of 34, he was appointed the first native-born Mayor of New York.

That same year he obtained a license to purchase "Lands of Wycher's Creek" (the Croton River). He made his first purchase from the Kitchawanc Indians in 1683 and continued to enlarge his holdings until 1697 when his estate covered nearly 200 square miles. On June 17, 1697, King William III issued a Royal Patent designating the estate the Lordship and Manor of Cortlandt. As Lord of the Manor he had absolute control over all fish and game on his lands, could convert the virgin forests into lumber and lease land to tenant settlers. These privileges cost him 40 shillings a year.

Stephanus, who died in 1700, did not adopt the English system of primogeniture, which would have meant leaving the entire estate to his oldest son. Instead he followed the Dutch tradition and bequeathed the estate to all of his immediate heirs to keep as a unit or divide as they wished.

There is no record as to when the manor house was originally built, but it is believed that the lowest floor of the present stone manor was standing when Philip's father purchased that parcel from New York's Governor Thomas Dongan. The first enlargement of the house was begun shortly after the death of Stephanus. Sandstone for the second story was cut on the west side of the Hudson and ferried across in the family work-boat. Red and yellow brick for the house is believed to have been imported from Europe. For most of this period the manor was used only occasionally by members of the family. When Philip died in 1748 only two sons survived him, Stephen who inherited the town house, and Pierre who received the manor house.

Pierre and his wife (Joanna Livingston) Van Cortlandt brought the house to its 18th-century glory. They had the interior plastered, added a broad porch and brought it many fine furnishings. Some of the furnishings in the restored manor date back to the 17th century.

At the top of the front steps there is a massive Dutch door which opens into a hall. At the right is the parlor containing examples of Queen Anne, Chippendale and classical styles of furniture, many of them family possessions. In the dining room across the hall many of the members of the Hudson River aristocracy were entertained. An imposing William and Mary gateleg of about 1680, with a mahogany top, dominates the room.

On the left, at the rear of the hall is the "prophet's chamber" — so called by the family since it was used when circuit riders, ministers and bishops came to visit. Across the hall is a second chamber with many of the small personal possessions of members of the family.

A long walk leads to the Ferry House and the Ferry House Kitchen. The Van Cortlandts rented these to tenants who operated the ferry. In the 18th century the ferry operator was required to have a place to provide overnight accommodations for travelers. Meals for the Ferry House were prepared in the Ferry House Kitchen, which is a one-room brick building with lean-to, containing a large, hooded fireplace. In the common room of the Ferry House travelers and local farmers gathered to refresh themselves and to talk over the events of the day.

The property remained in the Van Cortlandt family for over 200 years and in 1953 was purchased by John D. Rockefeller Jr., for the purpose of restoring it to the days when it was the seat of one of the most hospitable houses along the Hudson River.

Eight years previously, Mr. Rockefeller purchased another Hudson River Valley house famed for its hospitality — Washington Irving's picturesque

19th-century home, Sunnyside, at Tarrytown.

The house stands on a high bank of the river, but bears little resemblance to the 17th-century Dutch cottage which the famed American author purchased in 1835. Looking at it himself after he had made a series of changes, he described it as "a little old-fashioned stone mansion, all made up of gable ends, and as full of angles and corners as an old cocked hat."

Despite his rather facetious description, Sunnyside has a charm all its own. Beautifully landscaped grounds with flowers growing in profusion, quiet glens and sheltering groves surround the house. There is also a duck pond, which Irving called his "Little Mediterranean," and a waterfall. Nearby are the service buildings: the woodshed, root cellar and a steepled ice house.

Irving was a bachelor, but he had nieces, nephews and brothers living with him, as well as an endless stream of guests. Even after enlarging the cottage, he found that the house was still too small and, in 1847, added a three-story tower which he called the "pagoda" because of its combination of Chinese and Gothic elements. This area housed servants and any overflow of guests.

Through his diplomatic service in England and Spain he came to know most of the important painters, writers and intellectuals of his day both in this country and in Europe. Born in New York City in 1783, he studied law and was admitted to the bar, but his main interest was literature.

He began his diplomatic career on the staff of the American legation in Madrid in 1826 and during the next three years wrote *A History of the Life and Voyages of Christopher Columbus* and *The Alhambra*. In 1829 he went to London as secretary of the United States legation and remained there until his return to this country in 1832. Except for a four-year period, 1842-1846, when he was American Minister to Spain, he spent his life at Sunnyside after purchasing it in 1835.

His study, on the right of the central hall, was often the scene of lively literary discussions and the huge desk, the chairs, the massive bookcases, containing his library, are there today. Also there is a daybed in a draped alcove which was used by Irving nightly for the first ten years he lived at Sunnyside when the house was overflowing with relatives and friends. The parlor, on the left rear, was the center of family life. At the far end of the

parlor is a picture gallery containing many of the original drawings done by famous artists to illustrate Irving's works.

These two houses — Van Cortlandt Manor, the home of the aristocratic statesmen-merchants of colonial times, and Sunnyside, the retreat of one of the nation's great literary figures — form in themselves and through their occupants an almost complete history of not only the Hudson River Valley before the Civil War, but the fledgling days of the nation.

Above: Van Cortlandt Manor was once the 200-mile-square estate of New York City's first native-born mayor. Below: Travelers refreshed themselves in this room of the Ferry House at the river's edge of the manor where ferryboats crossed the Hudson.

THOMPSON-NEELY HOUSE
WASHINGTON CROSSING STATE PARK, PENNSYLVANIA

WASHINGTON'S HEADQUARTERS
VALLEY FORGE STATE PARK, PENNSYLVANIA

FORD MANSION
MORRISTOWN NATIONAL HISTORIC PARK, NEW JERSEY

Three Houses of Decision During the Revolution

The lot of the Continental Army during the first four winters of the American Revolution hardly led to any visions of an early victory for the woe-be-draggled troops who struggled through the snow and huddled around campfires.

One bright spot during this period came on Christmas Night, 1776, when George Washington, in a daring move, brought his troops across the Delaware for an audacious attack on the British at Trenton, New Jersey. The next winter, 1777-1778, found the fortunes of the Americans at their lowest ebb as they sat out the bitter cold at Valley Forge; and during the winter of 1779-1780 at Morristown, New Jersey, the intense cold caused much suffering and depression among officers and men.

These three events — each crucial to the Revolution and each a superb example of General Washington's leadership, patience and fortitude — are memorialized today in three houses, around each of which one of the events centered.

The plans for the Christmas Night attack on Trenton were formulated in a Bucks County, Pennsylvania farmhouse — the Thompson-Neely House — by Washington and members of his staff.

Brigadier General William Alexander, titular Earl of Stirling, who had sided with the American cause, was headquartered at the house which had been turned over to him by the occupants. It was here that Washington had to consider what would happen to his ill-equipped army if he dragged it into battle with the British in mid-winter. After intense talks, the decision was made — and the house became known as "The House of Decision."

The original section of the Thompson-Neely House was a one-room stone cabin which was built in 1702 by John Pidcock. The west end of the house consisting of two stories was added in 1757. A few years later a second story was added to the original part and, in 1788, the east end was built.

Robert Thompson acquired the property around 1748, when he married the widow of Robert Simpson. His daughter married a William Neely and both families occupied the house at the time of the Revolution. Descendants remained in possession of the property until 1880. From that time until 1926, when the Commonwealth of Pennsylvania purchased it, the property was privately owned.

A grist mill, built by Robert Simpson about 1740, and operated by Robert Thompson at the time of Washington's encampment, stands at the foot of nearby Bowman's Hill. It is said that Robert Thompson never turned a man away from the mill, even if he had no money.

Thompson-Neely House: Washington Crossing State Park, Pennsylvania. Open to the public. Color illustration, p. 67.

Washington's Headquarters: Valley Forge State Park, Pennsylvania. Open to the public.

Ford Mansion: Morristown National Historic Park, New Jersey. Open to the public.

Bowman's Hill State Wildflower Preserve is filled with the flora and fauna native to Pennsylvania and is dedicated 'as a living memorial to the men of Washington's Army. In May, the lilac bushes, believed to be over a century old, bloom on the grounds of the Thompson-Neely House. There is an herb garden at the east side of the front of the house and an old red cedar at the rear of the house which was 27 years old when Washington was here.

The victory at Trenton, where 900 Hessians were taken prisoner, and the following victory at Princeton did not spell triumph for the Continental Army. It did, however, give them the will to move without knowing the great difficulties they would face.

Washington and British General Howe maneuvered throughout the spring, summer and fall — with Washington always moving away from a direct confrontation. At Brandywine Creek in September 1777, and the following month at Germantown, Pennsylvania, Washington met defeat. The British settled down for the winter in Philadelphia and Washington's Army went into Valley Forge, the purgatory of the Revolution.

On December 19, 1777, the main force of the American Army encamped at Valley Forge. Washington had to explain his reasons both to his generals and to Congress. He wanted to be in a place which would not endanger the more fertile fields in Chester and Montgomery Counties to looting by the enemy. He wanted to keep his camp close enough to the "cozily kept" British so that he would be a constant threat.

Washington moved into the camp on December 19, 1777, and lived in a tent for a week. It was more than a day's march from Philadelphia, thus insuring against surprise from an overnight attack. It had the advantages that the rear line was easily defended by steep slopes to the creek valley and the northern line by the Schuylkill River. This left the southerly and easterly slopes of the valley creek to be protected.

After considering all the possibilities, Washington took his men into camp and a week later moved into the dwelling owned by Issac Potts, a young Quaker minister, and tenanted by a widow, Mrs. Deborah Hewes.

The building, erected in 1760 and acquired by the state in 1905, is located in Upper Merion Township, Montgomery County. Ninety per cent of the original building is still to be seen. It is readily understandable that the floors and stair treads have been replaced when records show that, for example, 384,377 persons visited the building in 1965. The tract of land on which the headquarters is situated was part of the original holding of William Penn.

It was in this house that Washington conferred with the Marquis de Lafayette, General Nathanael Greene, General "Mad Anthony" Wayne, Daniel Morgan, Baron Friedrich Wilhelm von Steuben, John Sullivan, John Peter Gabriel Muhlenberg, Baron de Kalb, Alexander Hamilton and others, talking over the problems of the Revolution, planning future campaigns, listening to the complaints of the common soldier — and addressing appeals for aid to the Congress. One such appeal came after his arrival at Valley Forge with approximately 11,000 untrained men. Four days later he told Congress that "2,898 men are unfit for duty because they are barefooted or otherwise naked." During the following months more than 3,000 died from disease, exposure and privation. By February 1, 1777, Washington reported he had only 5,012 men capable of going into combat.

This was the winter at Valley Forge when men huddled around small fires and often put their hats

Above: A room in the distinctive Thompson-Neely House is furnished in colonial fashion. On Christmas Night, 1776, Washington led his forces from this house across the Delaware to victory in the battle of Trenton.

Above: One of the finest examples of colonial architecture in this region, the Ford Mansion housed General and Mrs. Washington in the worst winter of the war, possibly of the 18th century. Below: Washington's Headquarters at Valley Forge from an 1876 lithograph. The house is situated on part of the tract held by William Penn in the 17th century.

on the ground to save their feet when they had no shoes. This was the winter of greatest trial and travail.

The general's wife made it a custom to spend a month or two with him every year and in the winter of 1778 she arrived to celebrate his birthday on February 22. Despite the hardships prevailing at the camp, this was the first known public celebration of Washington's birthday. Bands of various regiments and others took part.

Mrs. Washington occupied the second-story front bedroom of the headquarters. This room is preserved in the dwelling where she was a dominant personality of the camp. In her second story sitting room wives of general officers and women folk of the outlying farms spent many hours sewing garments, patching torn uniforms, darning socks, knitting outfits and preparing food and medicine for ailing soldiers.

Throughout the long arduous winter Washington and his staff listened to the complaints of those who wanted to go back to their farms in New York, New England, New Jersey — but he persuaded them that they would eventually attain victory.

Those who had prevailed at Valley Forge came to the Morristown area for the second time in December 1779. Washington's headquarters was made at the home of Colonel Jacob Ford, Jr., a prosperous iron manufacturer, landowner and patriotic Morris County militia officer who had died two years before, during his military service. His home is considered today to be one of the best examples of colonial architecture in the area. It includes handsome Palladian doorways, and two large chimneys serving fireplaces in the four rooms located on each floor off a central hallway. The two-story east wing contains a kitchen and buttery, with two servant rooms above.

At the invitation of Mrs. Ford, General and Mrs. Washington resided in the mansion for nearly seven months during what many consider the winter with the most severe weather of the war and possibly of the entire 18th century. Washington wrote in January, 1780: "Eighteen belonging to my family, and all Mrs. Ford's, are crowded together in her kitchen and scarcely one of them able to speak for the colds they have caught."

Washington spent much of the time at his desk still trying to find the means to feed and clothe the army, to encourage recruiting, and planning the coming campaign. But spring brought pleasant weather and welcome news. The Marquis de Lafayette arrived to tell Washington that a French army was on its way to aid the Americans. When Washington left Morristown shortly thereafter, he had renewed hope in the future.

MORVEN

PRINCETON, NEW JERSEY

On the King's Highway

When Morven was built in 1701 it fronted on a former Indian trail which, in the latter part of the 17th century, was known as the "Old Dutch Trail" and then the "King's Highway." Today it is the official residence of the governors of New Jersey.

Richard Stockton, born in England in 1645, arrived in New Amsterdam with his parents and numerous brothers and sisters 11 years later. In 1696 he left New York with his wife and settled in the wilderness of the Jerseys at Wapowog creek. The Stockton family was reputedly wealthy before leaving England and moved into the hinterlands in the pursuit of religious freedom.

Stockton built his home on a tract of land purchased from William Penn and it was a most unusual dwelling, considering its location far from the center of the major activities of the day, but the Stocktons, then Quakers, appeared to be prepared to build a life of their own.

The house is early Georgian in style, reflecting the influence of Italian Renaissance architecture which became popular in England in the 17th

Morven: U. S. Route 206, Princeton, New Jersey. Governor's residence. Open to the public.

Above: Constructed in 1701 by Richard Stockton, whose signature appears on the Declaration of Independence, Morven was acquired by Governor Walter E. Edge in 1945 and is now the official governor's residence in the State of New Jersey.

century, but it was still radically different from colonial dwellings — particularly those in a frontier-like settlement.

Although there is some question as to whether the present-day Morven resembles the early 18th-century dwelling, it would appear that the rooms of the central section of the house have not changed to any appreciable degree. However, the house was burned twice — once by the British during the Revolution and again in 1821. So it would seem that each rebuilding called for alteration.

It is also noted that the brick course of the two wings vary from those of the central section, suggesting different periods of construction. In addition there are variations in the building of the wings themselves.

The house that Richard Stockton built with slaves and indentured labor was constructed of native brick. It had a 45-foot frontage and was two-and-a-half stories. The doors, window frames, paneling, and mantelpieces were hewn and formed from logs.

In the 1830's Robert Field Stockton added second floors to the two wings and tore out the old wooden mantelpieces, replacing them with white marble shelves. When the house was restored the hand-hewn mantelpieces were traced and fitted over the iron fire-backs, which had never been removed. The garden was completely rearranged by Robert's wife, Harriet Maria, who had flower beds of geometric designs and trees trimmed into animal shapes. Today the garden, which had been copied from Alexander Pope's garden at Twickenham, England, has been restored to its authentic charm.

The plan for the garden was brought back by Richard Stockton after a visit to England in the early 1770's. Back home he gave his daughter in marriage to Benjamin Rush, a distinguished Philadelphia physician, and the ceremony was performed by a Dr. Witherspoon. Six months later all three were signers of the Declaration of Independence.

Richard Stockton's magnificent house was looted and burned during the Battle of Princeton and he was taken prisoner. Down through the years the Stocktons played a prominent role in both state and national affairs and maintained ownership of Morven until it was acquired by Governor Walter E. Edge in 1945, who left it to the state as an official governor's residence, a state museum or historic site.

For the first 50 years of its existence the dwelling was known as the Stockton House. Then in 1755 the grandson of the builder married Annis Boudinot Stockton. At about that time the Ossianic cycle of tales and poems was the most popular reading to come from England. She found that Morven was the purported name of the castle of Fingal, King of the Celts, whose son was Ossian, writing about the deeds of his father. Thus the new name came to this fine old house.

THE WILLIAM TRENT HOUSE

TRENTON, NEW JERSEY

Trenton's "Genteel Brick"

The Trent House, a brick mansion built on the shores of the Delaware River in 1719, has three times been the residence of governors of New Jersey. Colonial Governor Lewis Morris was the first chief executive of that state to occupy the house, leasing it from 1742 to 1746. Almost 100 years later, Governor Philemon Dickerson bought the house and resided there from 1835 to 1838. Finally, in the last years preceding the Civil War, the house was leased by Governor Rodman M. Price, a tenant from 1854 to 1857.

The house was built by William Trent, the first Chief Justice of New Jersey. In 1714 Trent bought 800 acres of land on both sides of the Assunpink Creek at the Falls of the Delaware. He acquired other holdings in the following five years and in 1719 had his new home constructed. At the same time, he had a township laid out and called it Trent's Town, later Trenton.

A pre-Revolutionary description of the house has been found in the *Pennsylvania Journal* for March 12, 1767, when its then owner, Robert Lettis Hooper II, advertised the property for sale:

"It is accommodated with a genteel brick dwelling house, 40-by-48 feet, two stories high, four rooms on a floor, with a large handsome staircase and entry, with a cellar under the whole building, and a court yard on each front of the house, one fronting down the River Delaware to the ferry, through a large handsome avenue of English cherry trees, and the other fronting up the river to Trenton."

As it is restored today much of the original structure remains. The "large handsome staircase and entry" of 200 years ago are still intact.

Strangely enough, although a most complete inventory of Chief Justice Trent's estate was made in 1726, two years after his death, none of his belongings are known to exist — with the exception of a two-tined steel fork with bone handle, and a small book on legal procedure. A handsome tall-case clock and several fine pieces of pewter belonging to his son, William, are now in the house.

Using the "true and perfect" inventory, the committee in charge of restoring the house were able to locate pieces approximating the rarer items listed. A great pier glass "with scallop shell gilt with gold," a japanned corner cupboard, a japanned tea-table and a cleverly combined card and tea table and escritoire, also japanned, are among the pieces now in the drawing room.

In the dining room a tall corner cupboard and another pier glass are outstanding. The notable collection of furnishings of the William and Mary and Queen Anne period, has been made possible by the dedicated work of the committee and by generous gifts and loans.

Particularly impressive is the dignity and beauty of the interior architecture: the wide entrance hall, the high-ceilinged chambers with deep cornices, the great corner fireplaces, the original paneling in the drawing room and the staircase rising in three flights to a balustraded landing on the second floor.

Although the original color of the woodwork had long been lost, in time careful research led to a happy selection of colors. In the drawing room, beneath layers of paint on the panels, a delicate gray was discovered, a fitting background for the fine pieces of black lacquer. A gray green in the dining room sets off the fireplace panels and the cornices. The chambers are a dull white to simulate the whitewash used on 18th-century plaster.

Trent had been a successful merchant in Philadelphia for many years before building his house in New Jersey. He emigrated from Scotland in 1682 and identified himself in business with the Quakers. At one time he was a shipowner in partnership

The William Trent House: 539 S. Warren Street, Trenton, New Jersey. Open to the public.

with William Penn and James Logan.

He was named a member of the Pennsylvania Provincial Council in 1703 and served until 1710. Although not a member of the bar, he was one of a group selected in 1706 to systematize the courts, and later was named one of the five supreme court justices. This is all the more remarkable when one considers that he was a member of the Church of England, while the government of the province was in the hands of the Society of Friends. He also served as Speaker of the House in the assembly.

After building his home in New Jersey, he spent two summers there and made his permanent residence on the shores of the Delaware in 1721. Then the governor gave him a commission in the militia and named him to the Court of Common Pleas. In 1723, the year before his death, he was named the first Chief Justice of New Jersey.

Below: Interior of Mount Pleasant, Scottish privateer John MacPherson's estate, declares the elegance that was a part of early Philadelphia homes. Flanking the fireplace, intricately carved panels adorn china closets and serve as false doors to balance the décor of the room.

A.J. Wyatt

Below: New Jersey's first Chief Justice, William Trent, built his house on the Delaware River in 1719 and surveyed a township which grew into the present-day city of Trenton. The house has since been the residence of three New Jersey governors.

Trent House

BARTRAM HOUSE
MOUNT PLEASANT
POWEL HOUSE
PHILADELPHIA PENNSYLVANIA

In the City of Brotherly Love

Philadelphia, as one of the major centers in the early days of the colonization of this country, attracted many wholesale and retail merchants, shipowners and scholars. Its historic aspects are known to every schoolboy who has ever studied the events that occurred there from the days of William Penn through the struggles before and after the Declaration of Independence was signed.

It is only natural that the affluence of the province clustered around the City of Brotherly Love should give rise to the building of gracious homes; of which the city has more than its share.

One of the houses restored for posterity does not, perhaps, fit into the category of "great mansions," but its many fascinating features and historic associations make it worthy of a place among any list of homes to be remembered.

Bartram House was built in 1731 by John Bartram, the famous American botanist and plant collector. The grounds on the west bank of the Schuylkill River are the site of the first botanical garden in America.

Bartram was from a farm family. He loved everything that grew from the soil and cared little for the grand life and "fashionable" things. He was born in 1699 and although he had little education he acquired a knowledge of physics and surgery. It was this interest in medicine which probably led him to botany, since the vegetable kingdom played a large part in the medical field in those days.

While still a young man he inherited land from an uncle and started a farm. In 1728 he purchased more land on the Schuylkill along with a small stone house which had belonged to a Swedish settler. In 1731, after his second marriage, he added to the house. The kitchen of the Swedish dwelling still remains, along with one room over it. The kitchen has a great fireplace and the rafters are hand-hewn. Those in the section built by Bartram were sawed. There are many doors, so that each room can be entered from outside, a feature of Pennsylvania houses of that period.

During the years, as the family grew, other additions were made to the property. The first Bartram house was but one room deep; and the datestone in the south gable indicates 1731. Other alterations were made when the peak of the roof was lifted and the whole house was extended towards the river, making the dwelling two rooms deep and greatly enlarging the attic. The date of the alteration is determined by an inscription below the second-story window:

IT IS GOD ALONE ALMYTY LORD
THE HOLY ONE BY ME ADOR'D
JOHN BARTRAM 1770

The house has wide floor boards, paneled walls and deep window sills so characteristic of the houses of that region in the 18th century. Many of today's householders would be attracted to the many closets and the historically minded may ponder in which one Mrs. Bartram kept the blue china tea set given to her by Mrs. Benjamin Franklin.

Benjamin Franklin was a close friend of Bartram and the American statesman aided the botanist

Bartram House: 54th St. & Elmwood Avenue, Philadelphia, Pensylvania. Open to the public.

Mount Pleasant: Fairmont Park, Pennsylvania. Open to the public. Color illustration, p. 69.

Powel House: 244 S. Third St., Philadelphia, Pennsylvania. Open to the public. Color illustrations, pp. 68, 69.

Above: Curiously fashioned Ionic columns were constructed into the front of the John Bartram House in 1731 as its owner, a self-instructed botanist, enlarged the small two-story stone building previously occupied by an early Swedish settler.

both here and abroad. The small Franklin stove which stands just to the right of the entrance to the house was a gift from Franklin. It is the only object which was in the house when Bartram resided there.

Bartram's second wife, Ann, was not too enthusiastic about his concern with the shrubs and plants he was constantly seeking. However, he persisted and, while continuing to farm, he became a noted authority on plants and flowers of the new nation.

The botanist began his collecting on his own farm and in the area immediately adjoining. Later he started to go farther afield into Maryland and Delaware. When he was 66 years old he made a field trip to Florida with his son William. His specimens he kept in a "Seed House" just to the north of the family home. Here again stone, which he cut himself, was used.

John Bartram was a true gentleman of nature, firm in his beliefs but quiet and unpretentious. In 1769 a guest tactfully questioned him after dinner about having Negroes at his table, and Bartram told him: "Those whom I admit to my table, I have found to be good, trusty, moral men . . . . The oldest person among them transacts my business in Philadelphia. . . ."

The Bartram House remained in the family until 1850 when the property was purchased by Andrew Eastwick who was also interested in the extensive gardens. After his death the valuable gardens were neglected, and in 1891, the City of Philadelphia purchased the 27-acre tract for a park. The house and the gardens are maintained by the Fairmount Park Commission.

In direct contrast is the house once described by John Adams as "the most elegant seat in Pennsylvania" — Mount Pleasant, an imposing estate on a hill overlooking the Schuylkill River.

This magnificent estate was built in 1761 by Captain John MacPherson, a Scottish privateer, and is still considered one of the finest examples of Georgian architecture in this country. In the forecourt two buildings flank the main house. They were built forward of the front of the mansion and placed about 40 feet from each end. These structures are two-and-a-half stories high, with dormers in their hip roofs. The buildings were used for offices, servants' quarters and various domestic operations.

The mansion itself is also two-and-a-half stories, but was set on a higher foundation. Windows in the basement are barred and set in stone frames and the foundation is of hewn stone. The main part of the structure is light yellow tan and scored in imitation of stonework. The corners have bold quoins of red brick and at the second-floor level a belt of the same brick extends around the house.

Large symmetrical windows are set off with keyed lintels of faced stone. The hip roof is set off with a modillioned cornice and is surmounted with a railed walk. The west front overlooks the gardens and the river. Both the west and east entrance fronts are particularly impressive.

The interior of the house is laid out with the spaciousness to be expected. There is a wide hall extending from west to east with a large stairway to the left. To the far right is a drawing room. The room has two entrances to the hall, balanced by false doors on either side of the chimney breast. Beyond the stairs there is a small chamber which is presently furnished as a dining room. Directly above the living room are two bedrooms, each with a fireplace set at a diagonal.

In the restoration considerable care was taken to provide the finest of 18th-century furnishings to give the house the appearance it had when it was an elegant mansion of colonial times.

Above: The kitchen of the John Bartram House has been pre-served as part of the original structure along with the room above it. The pewter and earthenware utensils were probably wrought by local craftsmen of Bartram's time.

In addition to his feats of derring-do in the high seas, Captain MacPherson also turned his hand to other pursuits after retiring from the privateering business. He appears to have given lectures in astronomy, written papers on moral philosophy, compiled Philadelphia's first city directory and designed a vermin-free bed.

His first wife, Margaret Rodgers of Boston, died in 1770. By her he had two sons and two daughters. In 1772 on a trip to Edinburgh he married a second time. One of his sons, John Jr., was killed at the siege of Quebec in 1775. The second son, William, fought with the British at the Battle of Monmouth in 1778 and was wounded. Late the following year he became a major in the American Army and served with distinction.

Benedict Arnold purchased the house in the spring of 1779 just before his marriage to Peggy Shippen of Philadelphia. Arnold was already in trouble, having overextended himself financially while military governor of Philadelphia and had to float a large mortgage. After his infamous defection to the British the property was seized and his bride and infant son were banished from Pennsylvania.

For the most part the tenor of life in Philadelphia during the days preceding the Revolution was that of hard work and somber existence. There were, however, examples of luxurious living and gracious hospitality. One of the centers of social life was the Powel Mansion on Third Street below Walnut.

Here Samuel Powel and his wife, Elizabeth Willing, sister of Thomas Willing, financier and partner of Robert Morris, entertained at some of the most glittering receptions and balls of the colonial era.

John Adams, after dining there, gave a glimpse of life in the Powell House: ". . . A most sinful feast again. . . curds and creams and jellies, sweetmeats of various sorts, 20 sorts of tarts, trifles, floating islands, whipped sillabub . . . punch, wine, porter, beer . . . drank madeira at a great rate."

Sarah Franklin, in a letter to her father, Benjamin Franklin, wrote: "I have lately been several times abroad with the General and Mrs. Washington . . . We danced at Mrs. Powel's on your birthday."

Washington, the Marquis de Lafayette, and scores of other well-known personalities of the day accepted and enjoyed the hospitality of the Powels.

Samuel Powel was born in 1738 and inherited a fortune as a young man. He went to Europe to enjoy it and apparently did. He witnessed the coronation of Queen Charlotte, met King George III and had an audience with Pope Clement XIII. He returned to Philadelphia with a love for Old World art and culture and in 1769 bought the mansion which was to exemplify that way of life in the New World.

In his home city he served as a councilman, alderman and mayor. He was the last mayor under the British rule and the first to hold that office after the Revolution.

Austere on the outside, the interior is filled with impressive paneling, solid mahogany doors, exquisitly carved mantels of large fireplaces, many-paned windows, high ceilings with plaster designs and a handsomely balustraded stairway.

At the time Powel purchased the mansion the entire block contained only four houses. The rest of the area was devoted to gardens. His own was filled with statuary he had brought from Europe. The garden also has a pear tree which bursts forth in white blossoms every spring — unusual in that the tree is said to be more than 200 years old.

The mansion remained a residence for nearly a century after Powel's death in 1793. But the ever expanding city soon took over and the once stately mansion became a storage building. It was at this period that the Philadelphia Museum of Art purchased some of the fine paneling and interiors.

When, in 1930, it was discovered that the house was to be torn down, a committee was quickly formed and the structure was saved. Since then some of the original woodwork and furnishings have been returned and much of the most exquisite silver and examples of 18th-century china have been brought to the restored mansion.

MANDEVILLE HOUSE

GARRISON-ON-HUDSON, NEW YORK

Across from West Point

The practice of granting huge proprietory tracts to a few wealthy men was one of the facets which slowed down the settlement of the Hudson River Valley in the early part of the 18th century. A considerable part of the region was controlled by the Philipse brothers who were granted patents on many thousands of acres in 1697 by King William III of England.

In 1737 Jacob Mandeville leased 400 acres at five pounds sterling annually from Adolph Philipse, the owner of the upper patent. On the land he built a farm and a home which is still known as Mandeville House.

The first regular church services in the community were held in the house in 1770 and were continued there until completion of St. Philip's in the Highlands two years later.

The house, considered one of the few worthy ones in the area during the days of the Revolution, was used as a headquarters by commanders of the Continental Army defending the east side of the river opposite the fort at West Point.

Mandeville House served as host to Marshal Comte de Rochambeau and to Generals Israel Putnam, William Heath and Robert Howe. Several entries in Washington's expense account indicate that he also paid a visit to the house. The house maintained its relationship with the military in later years as is shown in a letter in the library of the Military Academy at West Point which states: "Some of the younger officers are going over to Mandeville's to see the girls."

Mandeville House: Garrison-on-Hudson, New York. Private residence. Color illustration, p. 68.

After the Revolution, the state seized all of the land of the Philipse family because of their Tory sympathies. Joshua Nelson, son-in-law of Jacob Mandeville, purchased the farm and it remained in the Nelson family until 1840.

In 1852 the house was bought by Richard Upjohn, a prominent architect of the Victorian era, and remodeled along the then popular Gothic lines. In 1937 Colonel Julian A. Benjamin, a descendant of Peter Stuyvesant, had the house restored and decorated in the Dutch-English character of the 18th century. Miss Nancy Allan has owned Mandeville House since 1953 and maintains it today as a private residence.

MORRIS-JUMEL MANSION
NEW YORK CITY, NEW YORK
Mansion of Pre-Revolutionary Manhattan

The Morris-Jumel Mansion is one of only three pre-Revolutionary War dwellings which have survived the past two centuries on Manhattan Island. Situated on what the early Dutch settlers called Haarlem Heights, the site was redesignated Mount Morris during the period of British influence and then Washington Heights after the conclusion of the Revolutionary War.

In 1765, Lieutenant Colonel Roger Morris, who served under Generals Braddock and Wolfe during the French and Indian War, purchased the site from its Dutch owners and constructed the mansion as a country home for his family. They remained on the estate until the outbreak of the Revolutionary War when, fearing the loss of his property because of his English sympathies, Morris fled to England. He returned for a period during the war as Inspector for the Claims of Refugees under British authority; but when a peace treaty between the United States and Britain was concluded in 1783, he and his family resettled permanently in England.

At the conclusion of the war, the house and grounds were confiscated and sold by the Commission of Forfeiture. Through the next 25 years, the mansion endured a succession of owners, was renamed Calumet Hall at one time, and served as a tavern and way station for stagecoaches. In 1810, however, Stephen Jumel, who had fled his Santa Domingo plantation years earlier and acquired a new fortune as a wine merchant in America, bought the estate. Jumel died in 1832 and a year later, his widow married the aging Aaron Burr, Vice-President during Thomas Jefferson's first term in office. This marriage lasted only two years, but in the years before her death in 1865, she restored the house to its original elegance and established a tradition of social extravagance which became leg-

Above: The Morris-Jumel Mansion has been restored in both French Empire and Federal styles. At age 58 the widowed Mrs. Jumel married 78-year-old Aaron Burr, one-time Vice-President of Thomas Jefferson, in this tea room.

Morris-Jumel Mansion: West 160 Street & Edgecombe Avenue. Open to the public.

endary throughout New York.

Architecturally, the mansion is a representative of the mid-Georgian era, but later restoration required that the décor combine this period with the American Federal and French Empire periods because of the years and social origins which separated the Morris and Jumel families. The 19-bedroom house is comprised of two separate units, connected by a narrow passageway running from front to rear: The low-hipped roof atop the two-and-one-half story structure is capped on both sections by a small cupola-like terrace with a surrounding rail. Constructed entirely of brick with wood casements and quoined corners, a gable extends from the roof over the main entrance and is supported by four large columns beneath the face of the pediment. This last arrangement was unusual in that two-storied, columned porticos did not appear generally until after the Revolutionary War.

At the end of the main hall there is an octagonal room which Washington occupied as his headquarters when the Continental Army won its first victory over the British. Above this, a three-room suite served as Washington's private quarters during the period following Morris' flight to England. Included in the furnishings of this section is a folding camp bed of the Revolutionary War period. Also, a library on the first floor, which served as a nursery during the Morris residence, was transformed into a guard's room during the years of American and English military occupation.

After the death of Jumel's widow, there were years of litigation. However, in 1903, when the house and grounds were offered for sale as real estate development and the demolition of the mansion was forseen, a group of New York City women induced Mayor Seth Low to have the City of New York purchase the property for $235,000. Incorporated into the Washington Headquarters Association of the Daughters of the American Revolution, the mansion and grounds, under the supervision of the New York City Department of Parks, were restored in 1905; and an important historic landmark was preserved amid the skyscrapers that came later to dominate the New York scene.

HAMMOND-HARWOOD HOUSE
ANNAPOLIS, MARYLAND
Memorial to a Disappointment

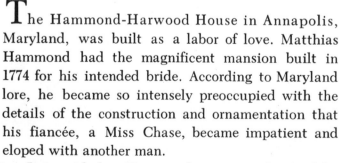

The Hammond-Harwood House in Annapolis, Maryland, was built as a labor of love. Matthias Hammond had the magnificent mansion built in 1774 for his intended bride. According to Maryland lore, he became so intensely preoccupied with the details of the construction and ornamentation that his fiancée, a Miss Chase, became impatient and eloped with another man.

It is said that Hammond was so embittered by the turn of events that he vowed never to enter the house again and rented it to a James Nourse.

Hammond was the youngest son of Major Philip Hammond, one of Maryland's most prominent tobacco planters. Young Hammond read law in Maryland and was soon deeply involved in the various patriotic groups then setting the flame of revolt in the colonies.

He was active in the Provincial Council, opposing tax laws imposed by Parliament, a member of the Sons of Liberty and the Committee of Observation. He also served on the vestry of St. Anne's Church from 1773 to 1776. But after only his 28th year, his name suddenly drops from all public records. He devoted himself to agriculture until his death in 1786. There has been speculation that it was the broken love affair which sent him into

Hammond-Harwood House: 19 Maryland Avenue, Annapolis, Maryland. Open to the public.

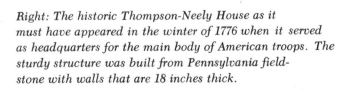

Above: The Council Room of the Thompson-Neely House in Washington Crossing State Park, Pennsylvania, was the setting for staff conferences which led to General Washington's momentous decision to cross the Delaware and attack Trenton on Christmas Night of 1776.

Yeager and Kay

Right: The historic Thompson-Neely House as it must have appeared in the winter of 1776 when it served as headquarters for the main body of American troops. The sturdy structure was built from Pennsylvania fieldstone with walls that are 18 inches thick.

Courtesy of Cortlandt V.D. Hubbard

Right: The reception room on the first floor of the Powel House contains some of the original family furnishings, including the silk fire screen to the right of the fireplace. Above hangs one of the few portraits signed by Gilbert Stuart, that of Anne Pennington.

Below: Mandeville's original Dutch-English character has been followed faithfully in restoration. The Garrison, New York, home of Jacob Mandeville served as headquarters for Revolutionary commanders defending the Hudson opposite West Point.

Courtesy of Nancy Allen

Left: When Philadelphia was the center of American government, the home of Mayor Samuel Powel was a gathering place and his wife, the charming Elizabeth Powel, was hostess here at lavish dinners and parties which included such guests as Benjamin Franklin and John Adams.

Below: David J. Kennedy portrayed Philadelphia's graceful and dignified Mount Pleasant in a delightful, hitherto unpublished mid-19th-century watercolor. The magnificent estate is still considered one of the finest examples of Georgian architecture in the country.

*Above: Throughout the turmoil of public and
political life, President Franklin Roosevelt often turned
to the gently rolling plateaus overlooking the Hudson River
and to the restful, refreshing surroundings of his
ancestral home at Hyde Park, New York.*

(Continued from page 66)

the comparative solitude of the farm after his few years of strenuous public life.

Mainly because of its fine harbor, colonial Annapolis was an extremely prosperous town in the mid-18th century. In 1769 a visitor said, "There are few towns of the same size in. . . the British dominions that can boast a more polished society." The house Matthias Hammond left behind was one of the most beautiful Georgian houses of the period, from 1750 until the Revolutionary War, known as the "Golden Age of Annapolis." It is still one of the show places of Annapolis.

The house was designed by the English-trained architect, William Buckland, who died the year the house was finished. It has a rather plain central facade, broken by a belt course between the first and second floors, but its simplicity dramatically sets off the exquisite doorway.

An entablature is supported by Ionic columns and has a triangular pediment and frieze of ribboned laurel. The doors and simple fanlight are outlined by an egg and dart molding. The spandrels are ornamented by festoons of beautifully carved roses. The central window over the door is more elaborately framed than the windows flanking it, two on each side. There is a richly carved bullseye window under the pediment of the roof.

The main section is connected to two semi-octagonal wings which conform to the lines of the central structure. The north wing contains offices and the south wing contains the kitchen and housekeeper's room and several servant's chambers on the second floor.

Below: While Matthias Hammond pondered every detail in the mansion for his intended bride, she impatiently eloped with another man. Embittered, he never returned to the house after that and it eventually passed to the Harwood family, the last private owners before it became a museum piece.

Edmund Barrett

THE WHITE HOUSE

WASHINGTON, D.C.

Home of Presidents

In the more than a century and a half that it has been the official residence of the Presidents of the United States, the White House has undergone many changes; some necessitated by fire, some to meet expanding needs, some to meet changing conventions and, during President Truman's administration, to save the building from collapse.

The main part of the residence is essentially the same as was designed by the Irish-born architect James Hoban, who was given the commission in 1792. The White House is the most distinguished residence in the United States and, set among trees and shrubs and well manicured lawns, it is considered the center of the affairs of the non-Communist world, as well as the home of the President and his family.

It is magnificent without being flamboyant. It is dignified, yet it has found room for the romping of children through its halls, as well as the more sedate pace of distinguished guests from all corners of the globe.

When Hoban was given the task of designing the residence, the commissioners for the Federal City expected that it would be ready when the Government moved there in 1800. However, when John Adams and his wife, Abigail, moved in they found the house far from finished. Abigail in a letter to her daughter said that lighting the rooms and keeping the fires going was a major task.

"The house is made habitable," she continued in her letter, "but there is not a single apartment finished. . . .We have not the least fence, yard or other convenience, without, and the great unfinished audience room [today the East Room] I make a drying room of to hang up the clothes in. The principal stairs are not up, and will not be this winter."

The White House was sparsely furnished; some of the pieces came from the President's House in Philadelphia, and the Adamses brought some of their own furniture.

When Thomas Jefferson moved into the Executive Mansion in 1801, he found the house "big enough for two emperors, one Pope and the Grand Lama." Jefferson called in Benjamin Henry Latrobe, a renowned architect and designer of the time, in an effort to complete the mansion. Latrobe modified Hoban's plans for the projected South Portico and added some of his own ideas for the addition, which was finally completed in 1824. He also designed a North Portico to provide the convenience of a sheltered carriage-way and also give the building a Classic Revival temple front.

Jefferson introduced a French and continental motif which was carried on by President James Madison and his wife, Dolley, until they were forced to flee in the summer of 1814 when the British burned and looted the mansion. The Gilbert Stuart portrait of George Washington was ordered removed from the building by Mrs. Madison and was the only object from the time of President Adams known to survive.

Hoban was recalled to direct the reconstruction of the burned-out mansion and it was eventually ready for occupancy by President Monroe. Congress appropriated a considerable fund for new furnishings and Monroe brought his own French furniture and silver for the duration of his administration.

With each changing administration, changing personalities and changing times, the White House took on some of the personality of the latest occupant. Furnishings were acquired from many sources and paintings, sculpture and silver were added to enhance the residence.

There were many plans for expanding the White House, but most of them were rejected. In 1902 during the administration of Theodore Roosevelt,

The White House: 1600 Pennsylvania Ave., Washington, D.C. Open to the public. Color illustrations, pp. 48, 49.

Above: The Lincoln Bedroom in the White House was a cabinet room in 1863. It was here that President Lincoln signed the Emancipation Proclamation on January 1st of that year. The two velvet-covered chairs flanking the bed are Lincoln originals.

there was a major restoration and enlarging. The main building was left intact, but the Victorian interior was changed to a restrained classic style. It was at this time that the separation of house and office functions was finally achieved with the building on the west side of a new Executive Wing, connected to the house by a colonnade which was part of the Jefferson pavillion.

Changes came more rapidly in the present century. The West Wing was expanded in 1909 with the addition of the President's present oval office. In 1927 the roof was rebuilt to create a third floor out of the old attic and the East Wing was added in 1942.

In 1948 it was found that the interior of the White House was unsound and the floors were in danger of collapsing. President Truman and his family moved to the Blair House and the entire interior of the mansion was removed. The old wall paneling and other details were carefully numbered and stored. A new basement and foundation were built under the exterior walls and a steel framework was erected in the interior. The paneling and decorative details were brought back and reinstalled.

Mrs. Jacqueline Kennedy, wife of the late President John F. Kennedy, refurbished much of the interior, in several instances drawing from furniture and paintings which had been relegated to storage.

During the Kennedy administration the White House took on a new aura. The United States was the acknowledged power of the free world and leaders from all parts of the world came to confer with the President. The Kennedy children had their play yard on the White House grounds and visitors delighted to see them charging about with their pets and their young friends.

In addition a new sense of cultural atmosphere was brought to the mansion. Internationally known musicians, painters, writers and theatrical personalities were invited to White House parties.

The interior of the White House has always been impressive, but in recent years it seems to have taken on an air of quiet dignity in keeping with the nation's role in the world.

The rooms on the State Floor, which is approached through the entrance hall and cross halls, have been modified since the mansion was designed by Hoban, but they still retain much of the original idea of the architect. The cross hall leads from the State Dining Room on the west to the East Room. The corridor is brilliantly lighted by two 18th-century cut-glass chandeliers.

The East Room is perhaps the best known room in the mansion. It is the first state room to be seen by public visitors and is the room where guests usually gather before a formal reception or state dinner.

Every aspect of the rooms on the State Floor indicate a flawless attention to detail of decoration and furnishings and each has its specific purpose. The upstairs floors are for the private use of the President and his family and contain accommodations which are in keeping with the family's position.

Above: This idealized bust of George Washington is a prominent part of the White House collection. Based on a model by Cerrachi, it was called "The Unknown Man" in the 19th century because people were unable to identify it.

The President's oval office in the West Wing looks out on the Rose Garden. The first White House garden was planned for John Adams. The Rose Garden was first planted with roses by the first Mrs. Woodrow Wilson. It remained essentially the same until 1962 when Mrs. Kennedy asked Mrs. Paul Mellon to redesign the garden and provide space for the reception of public groups.

The result was a traditional 18th-century American garden. The planting beds form the long lines of a rectangle framed by holly osmanthus and boxwood hedges. Each bed has five flowering crabapple trees placed at intervals. The plantings are changed from the early spring tulips and crocus to the chrysanthemums of late fall.

The garden has become a favorite spot for the President to greet Medal of Honor recipients, foreign delegations and groups of visitors. It has also served as the setting for a formal dinner.

There have been times, particularly in 1948, when suggestions were made to raze the building. But these have been rejected. The White House, residence of Presidents, is one of the most cherished parts of the nation's heritage.

READ HOUSE

NEW CASTLE, DELAWARE

The Reads of Delaware

The Read House, a two-and-a-half-story brick mansion, is in the style of the late Georgian period with profuse ornamentation and a facade that is broader than it is high. The main elements of the house front are firmly designed and simply disposed to form an energetic, assertive composition. Facing southeast on the Strand, the house overlooks the Delaware River. A lawn sweeping down to the wharf of the New Castle Yacht Club provides a delightful foreground for the mansion.

Work on the house was started in 1797 and was completed in 1801. It was built by George Read II, son of a signer of the Declaration of Independence, whose residence was next to it. The younger Read was a native of New Castle and a descendant of several generations of Reads who came from England. Read examined every part and detail of the work of building the house and frequently rejected what did not suit him. It is not known to what extent he may have directed the design, but someone's personality, probably Read's, has left its mark throughout.

It would appear that the Read family followed a pattern; they studied law, bought plantations, educated their sons for active careers to which law was an introduction and, like so many others of their era, took an active part in civic affairs.

The younger Read was a prominent jurist and was United States District Attorney for Delaware for 30 years. When Lafayette, the great French hero of the American Revolution, revisited the United States in 1824-1825 with much public attention, Read entertained him in the present house. Read spent 35 years in the house he had built and died there in 1836.

The house escaped the great fire of 1824 in which many of the older homes in the area were destroyed, including the spacious low-set mansion of the elder Read. In 1842, John M. Clayton, U.S. Senator and Secretary of State under President Tyler, came to live in the house for several years.

The land of the burned house next door was laid out as a garden in 1847, shortly after the property had come into the possession of the Couper family. They maintained it until 1920 when it became the property of the late Philip O. Laird. At present it is occupied by Mrs. Laird who has deeded the house to the Historical Society of Delaware.

Read House: The Strand, New Castle, Delaware. Private residence.

The front entrance is a generously proportioned doorway at the top of a flight of nine steps. Above the doorway is a fanlight and on either side there are tiers of glass panes which add to the light in the hall within. A Palladian window on the second floor is the same width as the doorway. On the roof there are two dormers set directly above the second-floor windows. The roof is low-pitched and hidden by a balustraded walk extending the length of the house, and chimneys rise in pairs on both sides of the structure, interrupting the gable ends.

One unusual feature of the house is the liberally embellished exterior woodwork, inconspicuous ornamentation hardly noticeable to the naked eye. The upper parts of the doorway and the Palladian window have been delicately wrought.

The same treatment was given to the interior woodwork where carved moldings, flutings, garlands and other details appear in ingenious variations. The first floor is divided by a broad center hallway. There are three principal rooms—the dining room to the right, the reception room at the front left and the living room directly behind it. The woodwork is painted white throughout with the exception of the floors and the mahogany doors. The frames of the doorways into the rooms are topped with paneled woodwork filling half the space between the top of the door and the 13-foot-high ceilings.

A large double doorway between the reception room and the living room has a crowning arch. There is a fanlight within the arch and it is divided into no less than 43 panels of glass which run in six concentric arcs. The wide-swinging mahogany doors are paneled simply, but the framework of the doorway is covered with lavish decorations.

Compared with the detailed ornamentation of this cultivated house, the garden's natural antique air is a contrast. There is the quoit ground where statesmen from Washington were in the habit of enjoying the companionship of the distinguished John M. Clayton during his occupancy of the house.

Below: Overlooking the Delaware River, Read House was built by Richard Read II, whose father signed the Declaration of Independence. The younger Read pursued a family tradition when he studied law and became a noted jurist.

DECATUR HOUSE
WASHINGTON, D.C.

The Ultimate Patriot

"Our country! In her intercourse with foreign nations, may she always be in the right; but our country, right or wrong."

These famous words of loyalty to the United States were uttered by Commodore Stephen Decatur in responding to a toast at a dinner given in his honor at Norfolk, Virginia, after his return from the Barbary Coast and the so-called Algerine War in 1815. The celebration was only one of many in honor of the U.S. naval hero who had secured a treaty with the Dey of Algiers and had negotiated with Tunis and Tripoli to end the piracy scourge in the Mediterranean.

Eleven years previously, during the Tripolitan War, he had won his fame in the spectacular recapture and burning of the frigate *Philadelphia.* A feat proclaimed by England's Lord Nelson "the most bold and daring act of the age."

Decatur arrived in Washington in January 1816, to take a post on the Board of Naval Commissioners. The 37-year-old commodore had received considerable prize money for his daring exploits and with this he purchased property in the city, including 19 lots in what was then known as President's Square, now Lafayette Square.

He picked a small area opposite the northwest corner of the square as the site for his town house and selected Benjamin Henry Latrobe, America's first professional architect, to design the house. Latrobe's name is linked with the three earliest structures in the square — the White House, St. John's Church and the Decatur House.

Decatur's occupancy of the carefully planned dwelling lasted only 14 months and ended in a tragedy that shocked all Washington and the nation at that time. He and his wife, Susan Wheeler, moved into their new mansion in January 1819, and the elegant house soon became the social center of Washington.

The social highlight of Washington in the winter of 1820 was the first White House wedding — the marriage of President Monroe's youngest daughter, Maria Hester, to her cousin, Samuel Laurence Gouverneur. The first ball for the bride was given by Commodore and Mrs. Decatur. On March 22, two mornings later, Decatur fought a duel with Commodore James Barron and was mortally wounded.

The duel arose when Barron, a suspended commodore, became angry over Decatur's opposition to Barron's reinstatement in the U.S. Navy. Barron was suspended for his conduct on the *Chesapeake* when she was under attack from an enemy ship in 1807. He remained in Europe during the War of 1812, returning after hostilities ceased. Decatur could have easily avoided accepting Barron's challenge except for the hero's sense of honor.

After Decatur's death, all the festivities planned for the rest of the week were canceled. Mrs. Decatur left the house, its carriages and all, and retired eventually to Georgetown.

The mansion, however, continued to be a center of political, social and diplomatic activities under a succession of distinguished tenants — first, the French Legation and later the Russian Legation. The diplomatic occupancy was concluded with the residency of the British Minister. During the years three Secretaries of State lived in Decatur House — Henry Clay, Martin Van Buren and Edward Livingston.

In 1842 the house was purchased by John Gadsby, a hotel and tavern owner, who lived there until he died two years later. His widow kept the property and leased it to a number of occupants, one of them being President James Polk's Vice-President, George M. Dallas.

Mary Edward Beale, wife of General Edward Fitzgerald Beale, bought the house in 1877. At this

Decatur House: 748 Jackson Place, N.W., Washington, D.C. Open to the public.

time heavy sandstone trim was added to the entrance and the first floor windows of the facade. Gaslight was also installed and the drawing rooms' floors were parqueted with rare California woods embellished with the state seal of California.

The Beale family was a properly prominent one for the house. George Beale, Edward's father, had won the Congressional Medal of Honor in the Battle of Lake Champlain, September 11, 1814. Thomas Truxtun, his maternal grandfather, had been presented with an urn by "the Underwriters and Merchants at Lloyd's Coffee House" for his action against the French during an undeclared war in 1799.

General Beale fought with gallantry in the Mexican War and later was the courier who brought the first official news of the California gold strikes to Washington. He also commanded a camel train from Fort Defiance, New Mexico, to the Colorado River, not a happy expedition. Army-trained mule drivers found coping with the temperamental camels so difficult that an amazing number of the animals seemed to slip their moorings at night and then were hunted down by Indians who preferred their meat to that of the buffalo.

The resilient Beale then became Superintendent and later Surveyor General of Indian affairs for California and Nevada and owned a ranch near the present city of Bakersfield, California. President Grant later appointed him minister to Austria-Hungary. On his return he divided his time between his ranch and Washington, where he died in 1893.

His son, Truxtun Beale, served as minister to Persia, Greece, Rumania and Serbia, prior to his marriage to Marie Oge in 1903. Mrs. Beale lived at Decatur House for 50 years and her supper for the diplomatic corps following the President's reception was an annual event.

It was under her direction, in 1944, that restoration of the house was carried out.

Below: Since Stephen Decatur built his Washington home, it has housed three European legations, three American Secretaries of State — Henry Clay, Martin Van Buren and Edward Livingston — and a Vice-President, George M. Dallas.

Edmund Barrett

BLAIR HOUSE
WASHINGTON, D.C.

The President's Guest House

The President's Guest House, more familiarly known as Blair House, is located within sight of the White House and actually consists of the Blair House at 1651 Pennsylvania Avenue Northwest, and the Blair Lee House next door, which has been connected to the original house.

The house was built in 1824 by Dr. Joseph Lovell, Surgeon General of the Army, and soon became a focal point for social and political life in the nation's capital. Ever since its first days it has been the scene of distinguished gatherings. Presidents Jackson, Van Buren, Lincoln and Taft were frequent visitors.

At the time of Dr. Lovell's death in 1836 the house was sold to Francis Preston Blair and remained in the possession of the family for over 100 years before passing into the permanent possession of the United States Government in 1942.

Mr. Blair, a Kentuckian, came to Washington to establish a newspaper, *The Globe*, for the Jackson administration. As an editor, he showed remarkable ability in his editorials to help mold public opinion. Almost immediately he became a member of that powerful, intimate group around President Jackson which came to be known as the "Kitchen Cabinet." His house, too, became a social and political center.

When Martin Van Buren succeeded to the Presidency, the intimacy between the White House and Blair House continued. Van Buren is said to have consulted daily with Blair. As the years passed, the editor's son, Montgomery Blair, came into prominence in the political life of the nation. The Blairs became active in the organization of the new Republican Party and President Lincoln named the younger Blair Postmaster General, and he became one of the President's most trusted advisors during the tragic days of the Lincoln administration.

The role of the Blairs was so decisive during the war years that they were considered as "perhaps the most influential family in the country." In a small room to the right of the front entrance, the elder Blair interviewed Colonel Robert E. Lee and offered him the command of the Union Army. Lee declined and returned to his native Virginia, later to accept command of the Confederate Army.

Twice Blair acted as intermediary between Lincoln and Jefferson Davis, President of the Confederate States of America. On occasion the war-weary Lincoln would stride across the street from the White House to confer with the Blair family.

The Blair-Lee House next door was built just before the Civil War by the elder Blair for his daughter, Elizabeth Blair Lee, who had married Samuel Phillips Lee, a cousin of Robert E. Lee.

Gist Blair, youngest son of Montgomery Blair, was the last member of the family to occupy the house. In August 1942, President Roosevelt approved acquisition of the house as an official guest house for distinguished visitors.

After President Roosevelt's death on April 12, 1945, it was the home of President Truman and his family for the first weeks of his administration. The Trumans moved back to the Blair House in November 1948, and remained there until March 1952, while the White House was undergoing extensive renovations.

The Cabinet had luncheon weekly with the President in the dining room of the Blair-Lee House and many important decisions were made in the President's study. It was while the Trumans lived there, on November 1, 1950, that Puerto Rican nationalists tried unsuccessfully to shoot their way into the house.

A priceless collection of portraits, cabinets filled with old china, silver and glass and English and American furnishings are to be seen in the house. Early American glass and silver, including a tankard by Paul Revere and old English silver and Loewstoft china, add to the interest.

Blair House: 1651 Pennsylvania Avenue, Washington, D.C. Not open to the public.

Above: Blair House, now a guest home for the President, has been a gathering place for distinguished persons since its construction. Below: During the Civil War, President Lincoln conferred with Blair family members in their parlor.

FRANKLIN D. ROOSEVELT HOME
HYDE PARK, NEW YORK

An Old-Fashioned Home

Hyde Park was the home of Franklin Delano Roosevelt from the day he was born. No matter where he went—to Campobello Island in Nova Scotia, the White House or Warm Springs, Georgia— he always considered the house at the edge of a gently rolling plateau overlooking the Hudson River as home.

The future President of the United States was born at Hyde Park on January 30, 1882, the only child of James and Sara Delano Roosevelt. At that time the house, which had been built about 1826, and purchased by James in 1867, was a clapboard frame dwelling. As a boy he played in the fields and learned the lore of the woods. It is said that he knew every tree and rock on the place.

It was here that he brought his bride, Eleanor, in 1905, and here that their children were raised. It was from Hyde Park that he started on the political trail that led to the Presidency of the United States. And it is here that he is buried.

The house has undergone many alterations since James Roosevelt purchased it. The original clapboards were removed and the walls were covered with stucco. The front of the house was completely changed to include a sweeping balustrade and a colonnaded portico. On each end of the old portion of the house two-story wings were added, creating an H-shaped structure.

This was the way the house was remodeled in 1915 by Franklin D. Roosevelt and his mother, and this is the way it has remained in accordance with his instructions.

The portico is well known to all Americans and to many from foreign lands. It was at Hyde Park that F.D.R. welcomed his neighbors and friends when he returned from gaining the Democratic nomination for the Presidency in 1932—and it was here that he was cheered by his Dutchess County friends on four triumphant election nights. Here he met the King and Queen of England in

1939, and later Prime Minister Winston Churchhill and other world leaders.

After the alterations of 1915, Roosevelt indicated that he wanted the house to remain as it was. Although he did not obtain title to it until after the death of his mother in 1941, his wishes were obeyed.

The family's way of life and the interests of three generations are immediately evident from the furnishings and decorations of the house. In the large rectangular front hall are a few large pieces of furniture and the walls are covered with part of one of the finest collections of naval prints in existence. Directly across from the entrance door is an 18th-century grandfather's clock and to the left of the door is a massive oak wardrobe. Both pieces were bought in the Netherlands by Roosevelt's parents while on their wedding trip in 1881. To the left of the clock is a sideboard acquired in Italy by James in 1869. The room also contains a wall case with many of the birds young Franklin collected as a boy.

The south hallway, just beyond the case of birds, leads past Mrs. Sara Roosevelt's writing and sitting room, known to the family as the "snuggery." The hallway leads down four or five steps to the large living room occupying the south wing. It was here that the family met, read and entertained.

The "Dresden Room" was so named for the delicately wrought Dresden chandelier and mantel set. An Aubusson rug covers the floor. The floral drapes and matching upholstery were added in 1939, shortly before King George and Queen Elizabeth's visit.

The adjacent dining room is dominated by a heavy, dark oak table, which could be extended to accommodate 20 dinner guests. A walnut sideboard, bought by James Roosevelt in Italy in 1869, stands to the left of an alcove and on the right is a large oak sideboard brought from the Netherlands in 1881.

The rooms on the second floor give more evidence of a comfortable, old-fashioned way of living

Home of Franklin D. Roosevelt Nat. Hist. Site: Hyde Park, New York. Open to the public. Color illustration, p. 70.

without pretense or ostentation.

In commenting on the furnishings, the late Mrs. Eleanor Roosevelt once said: "Many people in looking at the house will think the furniture old-fashioned, and they will be right, for it was good furniture when it was built and fortunately none of the people who lived in the house ever had the desire to change it because of some whim or passing taste. If one keeps things long enough taste usually changes and returns to them."

WHEATLAND
LANCASTER, PENNSYLVANIA

Bachelor President's Domicile

James Buchanan is not considered to have been one of the greatest Presidents of the United States. However, in the historical perspective of more than 100 years since his term of office, scholars are beginning to treat him more kindly and place more emphasis on the things he did do, rather than on the things he did not do.

He had a distinguished diplomatic career. After serving in the House of Representatives and the Senate he served as United States Ambassador to Russia and to England and was Secretary of State in the Polk administration before becoming 15th President in 1857.

His home, Wheatland, at Lancaster, Pennsylvania, was the scene of many political conferences during the desperate decade preceding the Civil War. Buchanan did not approve of slavery, but since he could see the difficulties the Southern economy would face if slavery were suddenly abolished, he tried appeasement.

Wheatland, away from the disturbing everyday turmoil of Washington, was an ideal setting for quiet consideration of the major problems facing first the candidate and then the President. The estate was given its name by a Lancaster banker who had built it in 1828 and was inspired by the fields of waving wheat in the immediate area.

Situated at the top of a gentle rising slope of generous lawns, flanked by tree-lined driveways, Wheatland is of Federal architecture, although there are some characteristics usually associated with architecture in the old South. The main section of the dwelling is square and is flanked by two three-story wings set back from the central portion. The main entrance is flanked by tiers of steps on three sides and the arched doorway is framed by four white pillars. The back side of the house has a long, informal veranda which extends the entire length of the central structure.

The high arched central hall runs from one side of the house to the other, with doorways on each end. Across the back veranda there is a view of green lawn and gardens as the landscape rises uphill; from the front there is a view of treetops and sky as the lawn slopes away from the porch, beyond the driveway.

Harriet Lane, the bachelor President's niece, came to live with him after the death of her parents and served as hostess at Wheatland. In the hallway is a staircase which rises to a level, off which another runs up to her apartment; the landing gives a view of the front hall and then curves up to the second floor.

On entering the house and being ushered into the formal drawing room at the left of the main hall, a guest is immediately conscious of the Chickering piano which dominates the room. This piece was purchased for Harriet Lane and was the center of the social gatherings at Wheatland. Other eye catching pieces include a fireplace of Italian mar-

Wheatland: 1120 Marietta Ave., Lancaster, Pennsylvania. Open to the public. Color illustration, p. 47.

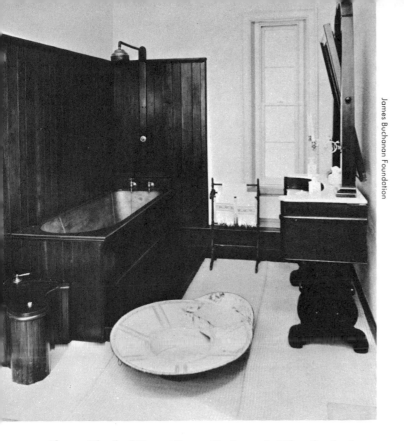

James Buchanan Foundation

Above: The facilities at James Buchanan's Wheatland, although primitive by present standards, were adequate, perhaps luxurious, in their time. Brightly decorated basin in the foreground appears to be a forerunner of the wood-cased bathtub and shower.

ble, formal draperies and venetian blinds, a magnificent chandelier of crystal prisms, lovely damask and velvet chairs and marble topped tables.

Adjoining the drawing room is a cool and quiet study which appears just as it did in Buchanan's time. There is a large center table, a small writing desk, a comfortable chair with footrest and shelves of books. It was an ideal place for harried leaders of North and South to confer and look out over the pleasant surroundings.

On the second floor, Buchanan's bedroom has been completely restored as it was shown in an etching in *Leslie's Weekly* in 1857, when he was interviewed just before leaving for his inauguration. Here hangs a portrait of Anne Coleman, a key to the bachelor life he led. Miss Coleman, a daughter of a wealthy Lancaster ironmaker, was engaged to Buchanan when both were young. It is said that the couple had a lovers' quarrel and that her family was, in any case, opposed to the match. Before things could be straightened out Miss Anne died and Buchanan vowed he would never marry — a vow kept until his own death in 1868.

WALT WHITMAN HOUSE
CAMDEN, NEW JERSEY

Order Amid Chaos

The house at 238 Mickle Street in Camden, New Jersey, has nothing to recommend it architecturally. The two-story frame structure with six cramped rooms was built for a lower middle-class working man of the mid-19th century.

In the 1880's the entire neighborhood consisted of working men, their broods of children — and one immortal figure, Walt Whitman. Here in his declining years he found peace and contentment, and while the distinguished personalities who visited him might have wondered about the surroundings, Whitman appeared to most to be unaware of anything being amiss about his place of residence.

He was at home among his neighbors, and the shouting and din of youngsters at play never seemed to interfere with his concentration.

Born in West Hills, Long Island, in 1819, Whitman learned the printing trade after leaving school and then taught in country schools on Long Island. For a short time he tried his hand at journalism but gave that up to undertake a long walking tour of the country. During the tour he supported himself by doing various work, mainly carpentry.

In 1855, at the age of 36, he published his first work, *Leaves of Grass*, which was highly acclaimed by the renowned Ralph Waldo Emerson. It is the poem on which his fame mainly rests, although he continued to add to this volume and do other writ-

Walt Whitman House: 330 Mickle Street, Camden, New Jersey. Open to the public.

Above: When Walt Whitman took over his Camden, New Jersey, home he had to furnish it with boxes for tables and chairs. Below: At 7:22 a.m., April 15, 1865, Abraham Lincoln died in the home of William Petersen. Despite many visitors in succeeding years, it was not opened to the public until O. H. Oldroyd displayed his Lincoln collection there in 1893.

ing for the remainder of his life.

During the Civil War his brother was wounded and Whitman went to Washington to aid him, remaining to work as an army male nurse for the rest of the conflict. After the war he obtained a clerical job in the capital. In 1873 he suffered paralysis and during his recuperation was badly shaken by the death of his mother.

It was in this period that he moved to Camden, living first with a brother, George. The arrangement did not prove satisfactory, however, and the poet scraped together enough money to buy the house on Mickle Street which had no furnace and was badly in need of repairs.

The neighborhood was not what a real estate man would call "a desirable location." The railroad was a block away and freight trains were banging and clanking day and night, sending soot and smoke over the area. When the wind was in the southwest a pungent odor wafted over from a fertilizer factory on the Philadelphia side of the Delaware River. The streetcars to the ferries stopped only a block away and this was a big consideration to the crippled poet. An attorney friend obtained annual passes for Whitman, thus enabling him to get into Philadelphia without cost.

When he bought the house it was occupied by

an elderly workingman and his wife. He agreed to let them stay on if they would board him. However, they soon found him monopolizing the living room and they could not put up with his irregular hours. So, they moved out, taking their furniture with them and he was left with an empty house. He somehow acquired a small oil stove, a couple of cooking pans, a few dishes and some wooden boxes for tables and chairs. At the same time his sister-in-law gave him back his mother's bed. It was not exactly an ideal situation but it did not appear to bother Whitman.

Then his fortunes — never very high — fell to a low ebb. In 1883 his royalties amounted to $300, but in 1884 they dropped to $42.77. In the midst of this he became acquainted with Mrs. Mary Oakes Davis, a widow, who became his housekeeper and remained with him until his death in 1892. During the last three years of Whitman's life, when he was ill at home, Horace Traubel, an editor and a close friend, also helped to take care of the poet.

The first-floor front room appeared to visitors to be a sort of office and a place to receive callers. It contained unsold copies of his works not handled by his publishers in Philadelphia.

An English visitor described his room on the second floor as partly carpeted and heated by a little stove: "All around him were books, manuscripts, letters, papers, magazines, parcels tied up with bits of string, photographs and literary material, which was piled a yard high, filled two or three wastepaper baskets, flowed over them to the floor, beneath the table, on to and under the chairs, bed, washstands, etc., so that whenever he moved from his chair he had literally to wade through this sea of chaotic disorder and confusion."

But Whitman could immediately put his hand on whatever he wanted in this chaos. His sense of order was in his mind and his poetry.

In 1920 the house was purchased from some Whitman relatives by a group who represented the City of Camden. It was turned into a museum which contains the original furnishings, pictures and memorabilia of Whitman.

PETERSEN HOUSE
(House Where Lincoln Died)
WASHINGTON, D.C.

House of Tragedy

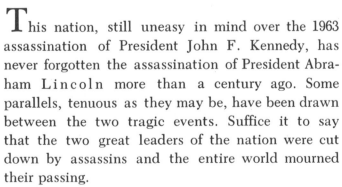

This nation, still uneasy in mind over the 1963 assassination of President John F. Kennedy, has never forgotten the assassination of President Abraham Lincoln more than a century ago. Some parallels, tenuous as they may be, have been drawn between the two tragic events. Suffice it to say that the two great leaders of the nation were cut down by assassins and the entire world mourned their passing.

Good Friday, April 14, 1865, was a brilliant spring day. Lincoln rose early as usual and was in his office by about seven. During the morning he met with General Grant and the Cabinet. Grant described his final drive of the war and gave details of General Lee's surrender five days before. Lincoln spoke kindly of Lee and other Confederate officers and said he hoped there would be no persecutions, "no bloody work," because enough blood had already been shed. After lunch Lincoln signed a pardon for a deserter. By four in the afternoon Lincoln escaped from his office for a quiet drive with Mrs. Lincoln. He spoke of their life ahead: "We must both be more cheerful in the future — between the war and the loss of our darling Willie — we have both been very miserable."

That evening, about 8:15, the Lincolns picked

House Where Lincoln Died National Memorial: 516 Tenth Street, N.W., Washington, D.C. Open to the public.

up Major H. R. Rathbone and his fiancée, Clara, at the home of Senator Ira Harris to take them to the theater to see Laura Keene in *Our American Cousin*. When they arrived at Ford's Theater the performance stopped as the Lincoln party entered its box. Lincoln acknowledged the c h e e r s as he dropped into the haircloth rocking chair at the rear of the box. A guard assigned to protect the President sought a seat where he could watch the play.

In the third act Lincoln was enjoying the play immensely as Mrs. Lincoln reached out and took the hand of her husband. Then the audience below heard a muffled shot and a scream from the box; a man hurtled to the stage shouting something that sounded like *"Sic semper tyrannis"* ("Thus always to tyrants"), the motto of Virginia, and then hurried off stage dragging his left leg. The man was actor John Wilkes Booth. The dying President was carried from the theater to a sturdy, three-story brick house at 516 Tenth Street, opposite the theater.

There, in a first-floor bedroom of the home of a German immigrant tailor, Lincoln spent his last hours. The house, which was the dwelling of William Petersen, his wife, Anna, and their seven children, suddenly became the nerve center of the United States as the long vigil with the President dragged sadly on through the night. Dawn brought a cold rain as Lincoln died at 7:22 a.m.

Life was never the same for the Petersens. A constant stream of visitors came to the door. Some wanted to see the room where Lincoln died, others merely wanted to talk about the assassination and the events in the hours that followed.

As early as a week after the President's death a Washington newspaper expressed concern that the "frail" Petersen house "would not stand long as a memento of the great man who died in it." The writer's worry was unfounded; the house has withstood the vicissitudes of time and the visits of hundreds of thousands of interested people. In 1876 the Petersen heirs sold the house to Louis Schade, an attorney, who was owner and publisher of the *Washington Sentinel*, a weekly paper,

The house was not opened to the public until 1893 when a Mr. O. H. Oldroyd brought his collection of Lincolniana from Springfield, Illinois, and installed it in the Petersen House. Three years later the Federal Government bought the house, but Oldroyd was allowed to remain in residence and exhibit his collection on the first floor.

In 1926 the Federal Government bought the collection for $100,000 and six years later moved it across the street to Ford's Theater.

The entrance to the Petersen House is reached by a semi-circular stone stairway with a decorative, wrought-iron railing. The front door is painted white and in the glass transom above the door the numerals "516" are painted in large black blocks.

The entrance hall is softly lighted and a somber tone prevails. At the left is the front parlor where Mary Todd Lincoln spent her hours of anguish during the long night of April 14, 1865. A wide double doorway leads to the back parlor with its beautiful dark marble fireplace, nearly identical with that in the front room. In the center is a marble-top table where Secretary of War Edwin M. Stanton sat to question and take notes from witnesses of the shooting. His portrait hangs above the fireplace.

Beyond the back parlor is the room where Lincoln died. It is furnished as it was on that tragic night a century or more ago. A large lithograph of Rosa Bonheur's "Horse Fair" hangs over the bed; Herring's "Village Blacksmith" hangs on the north wall over a marble-top commode.

A high-back rocking chair stands near the foot of the bed in the exact position where Secretary of the Navy G i d e o n Welles sat during the long hours of Lincoln's death struggle. The bed and the coverlet are of the same period and design as those which were there when Lincoln died.

Above: Pennsylvania Dutch baptismal certificate, dated 1807, from the Landis Valley Farm Museum,

LANDIS VALLEY FARM MUSEUM

LANCASTER, PENNSYLVANIA

Pennsylvania's Dutch

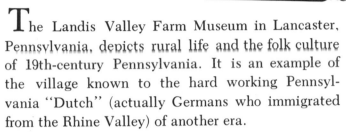

The Landis Valley Farm Museum in Lancaster, Pennsylvania, depicts rural life and the folk culture of 19th-century Pennsylvania. It is an example of the village known to the hard working Pennsylvania "Dutch" (actually Germans who immigrated from the Rhine Valley) of another era.

The first Landis to settle in Landis Valley was Benjamin who moved there in 1750. The Landis Farmhouse of today was built in 1870 and enlarged ten years later. The gray clapboarded house is an excellent example of rural Victorian architecture and is adorned with only a modicum of the "gingerbread" so often found in buildings of that period.

It was in this dwelling of today's Pennsylvania Farm Museum of Landis Valley that two of Benjamin's descendants, Henry and George Landis, began, about 1880, to collect those many items which interest young boys. They found guns, Indian relics, birds' eggs and minerals and painstakingly added them to their collections. At the same time their parents inherited old furniture and built up a collection of chinaware, pewter, quilts and other familiar articles of household ware.

From this humble beginning the museum grew, after Henry and George studied engineering at Lehigh University, spent a few years in the business world and then retired to devote their lives to the project in which they had so much interest. Over the years they brought together an accumulation of more than 250,000 pieces illustrating the early days of the Pennsylvania Dutch.

Except for the farmhouse, most of the Landis Farm Museum is not a restoration, but rather an authentic reproduction of the Pennsylvania village in which the contributions made by agriculture and farm and rural village folk to the area's history and economic growth have been gathered together.

The Landis brothers opened their collection to the public in 1925, but received little outside aid until 1940. In that year the Oberlaender Trust under the administration of the Carl Schurz Memorial Foundation came up with funds which helped in the erection of the Stone Tavern, gun shop, wagon shed and implement shed.

The farmhouse is typical of those in this lush valley. The front door is the double-type found in many parts of this "Dutch" country. One door leads into either the sitting room or kitchen and was in constant use. The other leads into the parlor and this one was unlocked only for weddings, funerals and spring and fall housecleaning when all the furniture was moved out onto the porches or the lawn. During the week the parlor was tightly shut, the shades drawn; it might be opened on Sundays if company came.

It is furnished in an array of American Victorian pieces: horsehair sofa and chairs, carved tables and what-not shelves. Appropriately there are plush-covered family albums, double-globed oil lamps, and heavily framed reverse oil paintings on glass touched with mother of pearl.

The sitting room and kitchen are in marked contrast to the stiffness of the parlor. These were the rooms where the family prepared meals and participated in reading and study, games and needlework and the spirited conversation which so tightly bound the members of the family together.

Another home at the museum is one built in 1814 by Jacob Landis, great-uncle of the founders. It is furnished in the style of the Federal period.

The big yellow barn standing amid towering black walnuts and locusts is always an attraction for artists and photographers. The old barn was torn down in 1939 and the huge hand-hewn timbers

Landis Valley Farm Museum: 2451 Kissel Hill Road, Lancaster, Pennsylvania. Open to the public.

were incorporated into this structure with dusky yellow sidings and twin ranks of many-paned windows set close under the eaves.

Inside the yellow barn is a series of booths containing exhibits of work by 19th-century American craftsmen and the tools with which they worked. Here are to be found such ingenious things as grain cradles, flails and wooden hay forks, manure hooks of wrought iron, a grain shovel carved from a block of wood, ice harvesting tools, a chaff cutter, a potato shovel, a pumpkin chopper—as interesting as today's mechanical wonders.

On a walking tour of the Landis Museum one will find a country store and post office reminiscent of the 19th century. The storekeeper exchanged his ginghams and calicoes, hats and bonnets, indigo and pewter plates, English crockery, spices, teas, coffee and chocolate, raisins and rum, for the farmer's dried beans and peas, firkins of butter and cakes of cheese, deer hides and the skins of sheep, fox, bear and muskrat and other products.

The Stone Tavern provided the farmer with a place to relax and learn the news of the valley, the county, the nation. Upstairs in the tavern is the Folk Art Gallery which reveals the Pennsylvania Dutchman's love of color and pattern and his lavish use of it in the most common articles. Gaily painted coffee pots, sugar bowls and marzipan molds, as well as cross-stitched embroidered "show" towels and samplers and a brightly decorated 1788 dower chest are among the intriguing items on view.

Also on the museum grounds is the gun shop, a reminder of the place where the famous Pennsylvania Rifle was made by Martin Meylin, an 18th-century Swiss immigrant. And in the wagon shed the famed Conestoga wagon holds the place of honor. This famed inland freight carrier rumbled over the roads of the East and South for many years carrying freight to coastal markets. This should not be confused with the later, smaller prairie schooner, which carried many Americans westward.

The conglomeration of early Americana to be found in the Landis Valley Farm Museum will give the visitor a unique sense of historical progress.

Below: The sitting and dining area of the Landis Valley Farmhouse reveals the warmth and simplicity of these spirited people. A parlor, separated from the sitting room by the entrance, was locked except for weddings, funerals and spring cleaning.

Above: Theodore Roosevelt's home was to be named "Leeholm" after his first wife. When she died suddenly, after the birth of their first child, he renamed it Sagamore Hill for the Indian chief who ceded the New York land to the first settlers.

SAGAMORE HILL

OYSTER BAY, NEW YORK

Residence of a Rough Rider

Sagamore Hill in Oyster Bay, Long Island, is exactly the type of house one would associate with Theodore Roosevelt. The rambling 23-room Victorian dwelling, even from the outside, is a projection of his personality. Inside, there could be no doubt as to the family who lived there.

One can easily imagine Colonel Roosevelt hurrying across the porch to meet visitors with his vibrating "Delighted" or "By Jove, I am glad to see you!" And then bringing them into his library with his renowned "This is bully!"

A delicate and asthmatic child from birth, he began a rigorous routine of daily exercises at the age of 12 to combat his bodily weakness, while an average consumption of three books a day contributed to his intellectual growth. Graduating from Harvard University in 1880, he achieved the finals in the university boxing championship, was admitted to Phi Beta Kappa and began writing the *Naval*

War of 1812. From this point, Roosevelt's career erupted in all directions, most of which is recorded or reflected in the 30 books and over 3,000 articles he wrote before his death. Within a year of his graduation, he married, bought 155 acres of land at Oyster Bay for his home, attended Columbia Law School briefly, and successfully entered New York state politics.

In 1884, however, this segment of Roosevelt's life was tragically interrupted. On February 14, following the birth of his first child by only a few hours, both his mother and his wife died. The next two years he spent combing the Dakota badlands for adventure, writing, hunting and ranching. Upon his return, he married Edith Kermit Carow, a childhood friend. The house at Oyster Bay, completed during his absence, which he had planned to name "Leeholm" for his first wife, was dubbed Sagamore Hill, after the Indian Chief who had signed away

Sagamore Hill, Nat. Hist. Site: Oyster Bay, Long Island, New York. Open to the public.

Above: Theodore Roosevelt added the North Room to Sagamore Hill in 1905 and displayed trophies from his world travels and hunting expeditions there. Sword and binoculars on Elk's horns were used by Roosevelt in the charge up San Juan Hill.

his tribe's rights to the land 250 years before.

Bookshelves lining two walls in the library are filled with masses of books on every conceivable subject and weighted down under the bronzes of animals and heroes. To one side is the President's desk where he sat when he received dignitaries and heads of state from the world over. It was here in August 1905, that Mr. Roosevelt met separately with the envoys of Japan and Russia before bringing them together a month later to sign the Treaty of Portsmouth, New Hampshire, which ended the Russo-Japanese War.

The parlor on the opposite side of the dark and spacious main hall reflects the tastes of Mrs. Roosevelt in its blue walls and white embossed ceiling. The books are the works of poets and 18th-century dramatists. This room is almost without the skins or hunting trophies which abound in other parts of the house. The only exception is the large polar bear rug, a gift of Admiral Robert E. Peary.

Gutzon Borglum, sculptor of the Mount Rushmore Memorial.

On a desk in an alcove is a statue, "The Puritan," by Augustus St. Gaudens, the sculptor who was called to Washington by "T.R." to re-design the American coinage in the Hellenic tradition.

To the right is a massive fireplace flanked by bison heads. These are symbolic of Roosevelt the conservationist rather than the hunter. He establish-ed 51 national wildlife refuges to protect species threatened with extinction. Other action came in the establishment of 148 million acres of national forests to halt willful destruction of woodlands, five national parks and a dozen national monuments.

The second and third floors at Sagamore Hill reflect the family's way of life. The children's bed-rooms are filled with gifts and souvenirs from all parts of the world — sawfish teeth from Venezuela, Philippine arrow heads, Zuni pottery, Navajo rugs, Hopi baskets and many other memorabilia of the worldwide interests of Theodore Roosevelt, rancher, historian, police commissioner, Naval secretary, Rough Rider, governor, Vice-President and President of the United States.

Wherever he went he always looked forward to returning to Sagamore Hill and the peace and quiet it afforded. He particularly loved the piazza where he was notified first of his nomination as Governor of New York, later to the Vice-Presidency and then the Presidency.

A story illustrative of Roosevelt's fierce loyalty to his country and his family concerns the manner in which he took the news of the death of his son, Quentin, during World War I. Shortly afterward, he had a brief statement for the press: "Quentin's mother and I are very glad that he got to the front and had a chance to render some service to his country, and show the stuff that was in him before his fate befell him." An observer who saw Roosevelt during this period, however, said that the "old side of him was gone, that old exuberance. . .the boy in him had died."

Today the spirit of Theodore pervades Sagamore Hill and here one can see and feel that he was and is (as stated in the Presidential Proclamation during the Theodore Roosevelt Centennial Year), "a prism through which the light of day took on more colors than could be seen in anybody else's company."

The North Room was added in 1905 and is built of Philippine and American wood — mahogany, black walnut, swamp cypress and hazel. When it was finished, Roosevelt took delight in bringing the best of his trophies to this spacious room. Across the wide antlers of an elk he laid his Rough Riders' sword, hat and revolver.

On the far wall, framed by gigantic elephant tusks, is the DeLaszlo portrait of the President surmounted by a gold eagle and wreath carved by

III SOUTHERN HOUSES

THE "OLDEST HOUSE"
SAINT AUGUSTINE, FLORIDA

America's Oldest City

The "Oldest House," located in Saint Augustine, Florida, is thought to have risen from the ashes of a primitive, Spanish colonial structure which was burned during an English raid on that settlement in 1702. However, archeological dating of the site's first occupancy reveals the presence of some dwelling early in the 1600's. Saint Augustine, itself, was settled in 1565, when Don Pedro Menéndez de Avilés was dispatched from Spain to destroy a French settlement at Fort Caroline in South Carolina. It is the oldest permanent European settlement in the United States.

As European interests in America expanded, hostilities between the countries expanded proportionately and the 17th and 18th centuries became a period of considerable turmoil for the inhabitants of Saint Augustine. Following a raid by Sir Francis Drake in 1586, during which the settlement was burned and plundered, English pirates again sacked the city in 1668; and in 1702, Governor James Moore of South Carolina led his English troops into Saint Augustine, destroying completely all but one hospital and 20 private residences.

English supremacy in Florida was confirmed in 1763 at the Treaty of Paris which concluded the Seven Years' War. Generally termed the French and Indian War in the United States, its conclusion gave Great Britain sovereignty in both Canada and Florida. English influence in Florida, however, lasted only 20 years before the termination of the American Revolution brought cessions from that country to satisfy a host of European enemies. Florida then returned to Spanish rule until Andrew Jackson, pursuing the British across its borders in 1814 and 1818, forced its cession to the United States.

The "Oldest House," as it appears today, is a combination of both Spanish and English influences, compromising the exact period of the house to about the late 18th century. Its first documented resident was Tomás Gonzales y Hernández, a Canary Island immigrant. It is conjectured that he acquired the property through his marriage in 1723 to the daughter of Mañuel Guevara, a third-generation Spaniard in the New World. During this period, the house was transformed from a single-level, tabby-and-masonry dwelling to a two-story building

The "Oldest House": 14 St. Francis Street, Saint Augustine, Florida. Open to the public. Color illustration, p. 104.

Above: The Spanish colonial origin of the "Oldest House" is evident in the rough masonry and adobe walls of the main room. The present building evolved from a 1702 structure, but the site dates to the early 1600's as a dwelling place.

which would facilitate defense. This addition may have been part of a general reconstruction following the British attack of 1702.

Hernández remained in the house until the British occupation in 1763, when most of the Spanish colonists were evacuated to Cuba. The British presence in Saint Augustine was marked by the destruction of many of the houses. The more substantial homes, though not destroyed, lost much of their Spanish character as the new residents made alterations according to their own traditions. It is believed that the addition of fireplaces and the substitution of glass for lattice-work in windows occurred at this time.

The next major change in appearance did not occur until the Spanish regained possession of Saint Augustine. At this time, the family of Major Joseph Peavett, Britishers who elected to stay after England ceded Florida to Spain, added an upper portico with a lean-to roof to one end of the house. The sup-

porting timbers for this portico later served as the corner posts for a first-floor apartment, added to the house around 1900. A large tower, removed during the 20th-century restoration, was constructed by Doctor C.P. Carver, who owned the house from 1884 until the turn of the century. He also refinished the interior of the house with intricate paneling from the neighboring Presbyterian church, razed in 1886.

In 1918 the house was purchased by the Saint Augustine Historical Society after their previous headquarters was destroyed in a fire. Dr. Carver had used the house as a museum for nearly a generation before this, so the society merely supplemented the collections it found there.

In 1959, an extensive restoration returned the masonry-and-wood building to its late 18th-century appearance, preserving in its architecture the conflicting European ideals which gave rise to Florida's violent arrival as a territory of the United States.

ADAM THOROUGHGOOD HOUSE
VIRGINIA BEACH, VIRGINIA
Jamestown: Britain's First Successful Colony

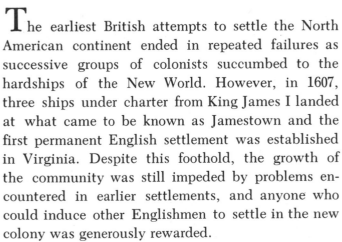

The earliest British attempts to settle the North American continent ended in repeated failures as successive groups of colonists succumbed to the hardships of the New World. However, in 1607, three ships under charter from King James I landed at what came to be known as Jamestown and the first permanent English settlement was established in Virginia. Despite this foothold, the growth of the community was still impeded by problems encountered in earlier settlements, and anyone who could induce other Englishmen to settle in the new colony was generously rewarded.

As a result, Adam Thoroughgood was awarded a ten-square-mile tract of land by the Governor and Council of Virginia when he led 105 colonists into Jamestown in 1635. The son of a minister, Thoroughgood embarked from England in 1621 as

an indentured person, but soon after his arrival, he was listed as a "gentleman," and in 1629 and 1630 he was a burgess in the assembly at Jamestown.

The home which he constructed on the west bank of the Lynnhaven River is a firm representative of the medieval tradition, long established throughout England at that time. The solid brick building was covered by a steeply pitched roof and embraced at either end by two T-shaped chimneys. This particular arrangement differed drastically from practices apparent in the New England colonies There, homes were constructed around a massive, central chimney and rooms were partitioned in such a manner as to allow a fireplace in each chamber. Originally the Thoroughgood House was built with three rooms, two on the ground floor, separated by a spacious hallway which extended from front to

Adam Thoroughgood House: 1636 Parish Rd., Virginia Beach, Va. Open to the public. Color illustration, p. 126.

rear, and a large, open loft on the upper level. A back door at one end of the hall which opened onto the river represented a New World innovation in Southern homes, accommodating summer breezes when the weather was unseasonably warm.

Thoroughgood installed a winding staircase of 17th-century design which led from the central hallway to the loft. However, this was replaced by another of Georgian descent when the loft was partitioned in 1745 to form the two upper bedrooms. During this restoration, too, the parlor fireplace was decreased in size, paneling was added, and the previously exposed beams throughout the house were covered with plaster. This was removed in 1957 when the house was restored again.

The exterior appearance of the house is dominated by the precipitous roof, originally covered with oak clapboards. Beneath this, three sides of the building are laid in brick with alternating courses of headers and stretchers, i.e. the alternating exposure of end and long faces of the bricks, each in a separate row. This manner of construction is known as English bond. The front of the house is more decoratively designed in Flemish bond. In this construction, the alternation of headers and stretchers occurs within a single row. The windows and doors of the ground floor are all topped with flat, segmental arches, a building technique peculiar to bricklayers in the 17th century.

The furnishings of the Thoroughgood House, like the house itself, do not reflect the hardships of the first settlers. As antique representatives of 17th- and 18th-century colonial America, however, their simplicity of design and enduring quality survive today as tributes to the fortitude and resourcefulness which brought them into being.

Below: Floral carvings were familiar decorative devices brought to the New World by European cabinetmakers. Right: Toby jugs, also in the Adam Thoroughgood House, were fashioned from English leather and used as ale tankards.

STRATFORD HALL
STRATFORD, VIRGINIA

CUSTIS-LEE MANSION
ARLINGTON, VIRGINIA

The Lees of Virginia

Two elegant buildings along the banks of the Potomac River, Stratford Hall and the Custis-Lee Mansion, hold unique and distinctive positions in American history through the Civil War period. For it was from these two buildings that the Lees of Virginia brought prosperity and government to the British colonies, fought for independence in the American Revolution and, less than 100 years later, nearly succeeded in destroying the Union. Now they are remembered here — as statesmen, soldiers and, above all, men of honor.

Richard was the first Lee to settle in the New World, arriving in Jamestown from England about 1640. He prospered in trade with Britain and rose rapidly in public affairs. His son, Richard II, secured a large tract of land in Westmoreland County and built an estate, Matholic Plantation. Just after this plantation house was burned by convict servants, Richard II's son, Thomas, established another estate at Stratford Hall. It was there that the Lee family began its role as an institution in American public life.

Even before Thomas Lee began work on the Stratford estate, he had been elected to serve in the Virginia House of Burgesses. This post led, in 1732, to his appointment to His Majesty's Council, a life-long post tendered by George II. With this appointment, he also became a judge in the colonial Supreme Court. By 1749, a year before his death, he became the first, native Virginian to be appointed governor. His most significant achievement, however, occurred in 1744, when he traveled from Stratford Hall to Lancaster, Pennsylvania, where he negotiated a treaty by that name. The Lancaster Treaty not only opened the Ohio River Basin to colonial settlement but assured the friendship of the Iroquois Indians when the French and Indian War broke out some years later.

The sons of Thomas Lee did no less than their father to maintain the Lee tradition in public life. Among the most prominent of them were Richard Henry, Arthur, William and Francis Lightfoot. President Adams once referred to them as "that band of brothers, intrepid and unchangeable."

Richard Henry Lee was among the first to implore the Continental Congress to dissolve allegiance to the Crown. Signer of the Declaration of Independence, he exhorted his countrymen to "Let this happy day give birth to an American Republic! Let her rise, not to devastate and conquer, but to re-establish the reign of peace and law." An opponent of slavery and supporter of women's suffrage, he proposed the germ for a league of nations in a letter to Lafayette, when he wrote, "Among the many leagues that are formed, why not one be made for the purpose of protecting human rights."

Arthur Lee, the youngest son of Thomas, was a prominent pamphleteer during the Revolutionary period. He presented the Olive Branch Petition which represented the last attempt by the colonies to make peace with George III.

William Lee was a London tobacco merchant and, although remaining in England, he stood firmly by the colonies in their demand for freedom. Following the successful conclusion of the war, he was appointed by the Continental Congress as commissioner to the courts of Berlin and Vienna to gain recognition of the newly won American in-

---

Stratford Hall: Stratford, Virginia. Open to the public.

Custis-Lee Mansion Nat. Memorial: Arlington National Cemetery, Va. Open to the public. Color illustrations, pp. 124, 125.

Above: The Lee dynasty of great public figures originated in Stratford Hall with the first native-born Virginian appointed Governor of Virginia— Thomas Lee. In later years, their championship of freedom was apparent in war and peace, in the United States and England. Below: Robert E. Lee marked the twilight of the Lee tradition. Here Union soldiers occupy his Arlington estate during the Civil War. A 1967 restoration has re-created simulated marble in portico pillars.

Front of Arlington House, June 28th 1864.

dependence and to negotiate commercial treaties.

Francis Lightfoot Lee was later eulogized by Mark Twain: "He did no brilliant things, he made no brilliant speeches; but the enduring strength of his patriotism was manifest, his fearlessness in confronting perilous duties and compassing them was patent to all...." A member of the Continental Congress, he too was a signer of the Declaration of Independence and, during the cruel winter bivouac at Valley Forge, he remained with Washington.

At the same time that the sons of Thomas Lee were gaining prominence in colonial and revolutionary America, a great-nephew, "Lighthorse" Harry, was also rising in stature. At the age of 19 he proved to be one of Washington's most capable cavalry leaders. After the war he served as a member of Congress and when Washington died, he immortalized the general and former President with the words: "First in War, first in peace and first in the hearts of his countrymen." Most significant, however, is that through his second marriage he begot a son — Robert Edward Lee.

An 1829 graduate of West Point, Robert E. Lee married Mary Ann Randolph Custis, foster great-granddaughter of George Washington, and the Greek Revival mansion which her father had built at Arlington between 1802 and 1817 became their home until the outbreak of the Civil War.

With the inauguration of President Lincoln in 1861, South Carolina ratified the Ordinance of Secession and withdrew from the Union. Apprehensive of what would follow, Lee declined the request to take command of the Union Army, explaining that "though opposed to secession and deprecating war, I could take no part in an invasion of the Southern states." When Virginia ratified the secession ordinance, Lee resigned his commission and returned to Virginia, declaring that "save in defense of my native state, I never desire to draw my sword again."

Lee did draw his sword again, in defense of Virginia and the entire South, as he assumed command of the Army of the Confederacy. For nearly three years he outmaneuvered and outfought the superior forces of the Union; but when an obscure Union officer from Illinois took a determined hold on the Western extension of Lee's army and moved diligently eastward, consuming the Confederate forces on every ground, Lee's fate was sealed. On April 9, 1865, he surrendered to the commander of the Union Army, General Ulysses S. Grant.

Lee never returned to Arlington after his departure in 1861. The Union army established a garrison there from which to defend Washington and, in 1864, the estate was seized for a national cemetery.

Separated by nearly a hundred miles, both Lee houses overlook the Potomac River outside of Washington. Stratford Hall, with its red brick laid in Flemish bond and palatial exterior staircases of corbeled stone, remains a fine example of early American Georgian architecture. Most striking and, perhaps, unique about this structure are the two chimney groups, rising at opposing ends of the

Above: This silver tea urn from the Custis collection at Mount Vernon was wrought prior to the death of Daniel Parke Custis, Martha Washington's first husband. The urn is engraved with the Custis coat of arms.

house. Each group is comprised of four separate stacks, joined by arches, to form small pavilions above the short, hipped roof.

The Custis-Lee Mansion looks out over Arlington National Cemetery, reflecting the changing architectural, as well as political, influences. A classic among the Greek Revival designs popular through the Atlantic seaboard and Southern states before the Civil War, the Custis-Lee Mansion is comprised of a large central unit, adjoined by two opposing and smaller wings. The pitched roof of the building's main element is dominated by a graceful pediment and supporting Doric columns which stand at the top of expansive, temple-like stairs. Built almost entirely of brick, all exterior walls were covered with heavy, protective plaster and deeply scored to give the impression of cut stone.

Since the turn of the century, both Stratford Hall and the Custis-Lee Mansion have been restored, preserving the memory of one of the greatest and most beloved military leaders of all time. However, most important about this man who nearly succeeded in saving the Confederacy is not his course of action but the quality of the decision that moved him. For that is how the Lees of Virginia are remembered — as statesmen, soldiers, and above all, men of honor.

MOUNT VERNON
VIRGINIA

Washington's Happy Reward

"No estate in United America is more pleasantly situated than this. It lies in a high, dry and healthy country 300 miles by water from the sea."

Thus George Washington described the estate of Mount Vernon in a letter to an English correspondent. Time and circumstance have done little to change the Mount Vernon he so described. It stands as a monument to the builder, "pleasantly situated" on a commanding eminence overlooking the Potomac and the low Maryland hills.

In 1740, Augustine Washington, father of George, deeded the Huntington Creek Plantation, which he had bought in 1726 from his sister and her husband, to his son Lawrence, elder half-brother of George, who had just come of age. In 1743 Lawrence married and settled on his plantation, renaming it "Mount Vernon," in honor of Admiral Vernon, under whom he had served in the Caribbean. Augustine Washington died in 1743 and his young son George spent a part of his youth with his elder half-brother at Mount Vernon.

Lawrence Washington died in 1752 and two years later the Mount Vernon title passed to George.

During the next five years active military preparations against the French and Indians kept the young proprietor away from his plantation.

George Washington and Martha Custis, widow of Daniel Parke Custis, were married in January 1759 and took up their residence at Mount Vernon in the spring of that year. Here they lived the peaceful lives of Southern planters for 15 years.

In 1775 Washington was a delegate to the Second Continental Congress in Philadelphia. That body appointed him Commander-in-Chief of the Continental Army and he proceeded at once to take command. Six years passed before he again saw Mount Vernon, and then it was only to pause briefly en route to and from Yorktown in the fall of 1781. In December 1783, he tendered his resignation to Congress at Annapolis and, turning homeward, arrived home on Christmas Eve.

The dwelling acquired by George Washington after the death of his elder half-brother was of modest size and typical of its locality and period. It was one-and-a-half stories high, with a central hall and four small rooms on the first floor; above were

Mount Vernon: Mount Vernon, Virginia. Open to the public. Color illustrations, pp. 104, 105.

dormered chambers in a corresponding plan.

In 1759 Mount Vernon acquired a mistress and the house was raised from one-and-a-half to two-and-a-half stories and extensively redecorated.

Mount Vernon as we see it today was planned by Washington before the Revolution. During the war the work was carried on by his manager and relative, Lund Washington. The mansion house was once again enlarged and embellished; small wing buildings were replaced by the present structures; the gardens were extended. After his return in 1783 Washington carried the plan to completion.

In 1789 General Washington became the first President of the United States, and except for brief periods he was away from home for eight years.

Mount Vernon is an outstanding example of colonial architecture. It is unique in many ways and owes its charm more to harmony of composition than to the beauty of its component parts. Washington had access to 18th-century English books on the design of country houses; the Palladian window and other details of the house, exterior and interior, were copied or derived from one or more of these books. Many artisans were employed at Mount Vernon, but it is apparent that the development and planning was the province of its master.

The most striking architectural feature of the mansion is the high-columned piazza, extending the full length of the house. It seems to be a complete innovation, and would, in itself, entitle Washington to distinction among architects.

In Washington's day, the Mount Vernon estate of over 8,000 acres was divided into five farms, each a complete unit, with its overseer, workers, livestock, equipment and buildings. Washington was one of the most progressive farmers of his day, despite the major diversions created by his public service. He corresponded with leading agriculturalists and was a keen observer of crops and planting methods on his travels.

The five outlying farms no longer exist. They were divided by the terms of Washington's will and since then they have disappeared.

The Mansion House Farm was not a farm in the usual sense of the word. The area about the manor house was developed as a gentleman's country seat, a New World version of the English country house of the period. Within a deep border of woods were meadows, vistas and groves of trees. Between the mansion and the river shore was an extensive park; below the kitchen garden was an enclosed vineyard.

The landscaped area of gardens and lawns about the mansion is separated from the surrounding fields on three sides by sunken walls or "ha-haws." The bowling green entrance and flanking "ha-haw" walls mark the boundary on the west between the formal and informal areas.

Perhaps Washington's attachment to his Mount Vernon was most movingly expressed in his famous Farewell Address of September 19, 1796, as he left the Presidency to return once more to his home: "Relying on its kindness in this as in other things, and actuated by that fervent love towards it which is so natural to a man who views in it the native soil of himself and his progenitors for several generations; I anticipate with pleasing expectation that retreat in which I promise myself to realize ... the sweet enjoyment of partaking ... the benign influence of good laws under a free government ... and the happy reward ... of our mutual cares, labors and dangers."

During the half-century following Washington's death in 1799, Mount Vernon's owners were unable to maintain its buildings and grounds. Neither the State of Virginia nor the Federal Government expressed an interest in the property. But in 1853, just as it looked as if the estate might crumble into ruins, a woman from South Carolina, Ann Pamela Cunningham, became interested in its preservation and devoted the next 21 years of her life to the project. To her and the Mount Vernon Ladies' Association, which maintains it today, is due the credit for saving Washington's home.

This organization has refurnished the house with period pieces; but year after year, through bequest, purchase and donation, the furnishings that were at Mount Vernon in the time of Washington are being acquired. At the present time most of the pieces on the first floor and all of the furnishings in the master bedroom are original.

GEORGE WYTHE HOUSE
WILLIAMSBURG, VIRGINIA

Witness to History

The George Wythe House on Williamsburg's Palace Green is named for its famed 18th-century occupant, lawyer and scholar George Wythe. It is a particularly fine example of a Virginia colonial dwelling — grand in manner but without pretentious ornament. Now restored and furnished as a typical 18th-century urban Virginia residence of a gentleman of means, this original Georgian mansion is today one of the major exhibition buildings in Colonial Williamsburg.

Considered to be Williamsburg's most handsome dwelling, the stately brick house was built about 1752 by Virginia planter and architect Richard Taliaferro. In 1755 his daughter married young attorney George Wythe and the couple took up residence in the Palace Street house. There, for the next 36 years, Wythe was to play host to many of the patriotic leaders who, like Wythe himself, helped to guide Virginia through the difficult years of the Revolution. Few houses in Williamsburg have been the scene and witness of more history.

George Wythe's public career spanned a decisive half-century of American life. A prominent attorney, legislator, scholar and teacher of law, Wythe fought long and hard for independence, the protection of individual liberties and the authority of the courts during the formative years of the new republic. He was first among Virginia's signers of the Declaration of Independence.

Like its eminent occupant, the Wythe House had its place in the American Revolution. George Washington, Wythe's client and friend, dined with

George Wythe House: Palace Street, Williamsburg, Virginia. Open to the public.

Below: The southeast bedroom of the Wythe House was occupied by such distinguished guests as George Washington and Thomas Jefferson. Among the first Virginia signers of the Declaration of Independence, Wythe also tutored Jefferson in law.

Colonial Williamsburg

the Wythes in their home on several occasions during 1769. Following the siege of Yorktown, the Wythe residence served as a military headquarters for the French commander, Rochambeau.

Another distinguished statesman and future President who frequented the Wythe House was Thomas Jefferson. Wythe tutored many of the most brilliant legal minds of the time in his home, and Jefferson was among the brightest students. In 1776, ten years after Jefferson's association with the house as a law student, he and Mrs. Jefferson occupied the dwelling while he was in Williamsburg to attend a meeting of the House of Delegates.

Governor Francis Fauquier, the urbane and admired governor of the Virginia Colony, frequently strolled down to the house for a nightcap. Fauquier, Wythe, Jefferson and William Small, a William and Mary mathematics professor, often dined together at the Governor's Palace or at Wythe's house, holding philosophical conversations.

In 1789 George Wythe was appointed Judge Chancellor of the High Court of Chancery of Virginia, and in 1791 moved to Richmond. The property was put up for sale and passed through the hands of many owners.

Spacious but simple, the high-ceilinged mansion has the characteristic symmetry of colonial dwellings. Two rooms on each side flank the ample central hall both on the first and second floors. Two large chimneys rise between the paired rooms on either side of the hallway, affording fireplaces in all eight corner rooms. The smaller windows in the second story have the same number of panes as those on the first floor, a device employed by the architect to improve the structure's scale.

The house has been refurnished with the guidance of inventories of similar houses, since no inventory of its furnishings was ever found. Antiques of American origin predominate. Styles of the late 18th century, combined with earlier pieces, show the English influence on colonial cabinetmakers.

The layout of the grounds surrounding the Wythe House suggests a miniature plantation. Fruits and vegetable gardens along one side of the central mall balance the various service buildings along the other. Behind the house extends a pleasure garden.

TRYON PALACE
NEW BERN, NORTH CAROLINA

An Old World Palace in the New World

Tryon Palace, described as "the most beautiful building in the colonial Americas," dramatically portrays American history. Construction of the original, large edifice and its two wings was begun in 1767 and finished in 1770, under the supervision of John Hawks, English master builder, "the first professional architect to remain in America."

Its architecture was unique in the New World in that it was designed as a London vicinity house "in the pure English taste," and served not only as the colonial capitol but also as the governor's residence.

The first Royal Governor to occupy the mansion was William Tryon, who had obtained appropriations of about $75,000 for its erection from the Colonial Assembly. He was succeeded as the colony's chief executive in 1771 by Josiah Martin, who contracted with Hawks to build a smoke house, poultry house and dovecote on the palace grounds.

Tryon Palace was the scene of the inauguration of Governor Richard Caswell and other state officials elected under the first constitution of the independent State of North Carolina in 1777. The first State General Assembly convened in this first capi-

---

Tryon Palace: New Bern, North Carolina. Open to the public. Color illustration, p. 123.

SOUTHERN HOUSES

Above: The brilliant color of blooming tulips accents D'Evereux in Natchez. A truly outstanding example of traditional Southern Greek Revival architecture, the home was named after the famous General D'Evereux, an aide to South American patriot Simón Bolívar.

Above: The "Oldest House" in St. Augustine was first a crude structure of palm thatch and wood. Evolved from its early form, the composite fabrics of the building manifest a long and colorful past, dating from its first occupancy in the early 1600's.

Right: In the Nelly Custis bedroom at Mount Vernon is the delicate crib given by Martha Washington to her youngest granddaughter, Nelly Custis Lewis, on the occasion of the birth of her first child in the fall of 1799.

Left: The graceful miniatures at Mount Vernon form an important part of the museum's portrait collection. This soft likeness of Martha Washington was done by Charles Willson Peale, who was not only a skilled painter, but an ardent revolutionary.

Above: The formal restoration area at Mount Vernon with the Potomac in the background. In 1798 a Polish patriot who served in the Revolutionary Army wrote, "The whole plantation, the garden and the rest prove well that a man born with natural taste may guess a beauty...."

Left: Unique in its concept of design and in the many innovations of the home and surrounding buildings, Monticello, the three-story, 35-room mansion of Thomas Jefferson near Charlottesville, Virginia, was the product of his own architectural genius.

Below: The distinguished statesman, Henry Clay, christened his Lexington home Ashland because of a surrounding forest of the majestic trees. According to tradition, the house was designed by Benjamin Latrobe, who helped design the Capitol in Washington, D. C.

(Continued from page 102)

tol of the state, and other assembly meetings were held there as late as 1794 when the state capital was moved permanently to Raleigh, North Carolina.

President George Washington was entertained at a banquet and ball in the palace in April 1791, along with many other distinguished persons.

The main building was destroyed by fire in 1798. Through trusts and bequests of the late Mrs. James Edwin Latham of Greensboro, a native of New Bern, the restoration of the palace was begun in 1952. Under the guidance of the plan John Hawks had used, the central structure and the east wing have been authentically reconstructed on their original foundations. Extensive historical and physical research has been put into the detailed and accurate redecoration of the palace.

From England came much of the 19th-century material, such as the beautiful mantels on the two principal floors in the central building; brass locks for the mahogany doors in that building; woodwork in the parlor, library and dressing room; doorways in the dining room and upstairs room; urns and stone baskets for the landscaped grounds; and the 1741 wrought-iron gate and railing at the palace approach.

Furnished throughout with genuine 18th-century antiques, mostly predating 1770, the restored palace is almost a shrine for connoisseurs of early furniture,

silver, porcelain, pottery, pewter, paintings, prints, maps, books, textiles, carpets and the accessories of 27 large fireplaces.

Besides reconstructing the smoke house, poultry house, dovecote and other houses, the Tryon Palace Commission, headed by Mrs. John A. Kellenberger, Mrs. Latham's daughter, has restored other houses in the complex which are now being furnished with rare antiques. The Tryon Palace gardens, designed in the manner of the 18th-century gardens in England, feature a section dedicated to Mrs. Latham.

The style and beauty of the Tryon Palace grounds are elegantly reflected in the Royal Coat of Arms of King George III, which is on the large white pediment at the top of the exterior north front of the palace. George III was monarch of Great Britain when the palace was built as the seat of the British government in North Carolina.

Made of elaborately carved and emblazoned mahogany, the huge escutcheon of the House of Hanover is the central feature on the coat of arms. Lions support the shield on either side; the Royal helmet with a large, jeweled crown is topped by a small, jeweled lion. At the sides are ornate placings of the red and white rose of England, the purple thistle of Scotland and the green shamrock of Ireland. Two mottos are included: "Shame be to him who evil thinks" and "God and my right." Both are fitting for a house of such grandeur.

SINGLE BROTHERS HOUSE
OLD SALEM, NORTH CAROLINA

The Salem Single Brothers

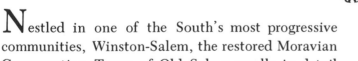

Nestled in one of the South's most progressive communities, Winston-Salem, the restored Moravian Congregation Town of Old Salem recalls in detail an unusual community during its vital years between 1766 and 1830.

The Moravian Church is the common name given in England and America to the renewed *Unitas Fratrum* or Church of the Brethren, which developed out of an association of religious reform-

ers organized in 1457 in Bohemia. Developing a system of primitive Christianity based on Scripture, the *Unitas Fratrum* flourished in Bohemia, Moravia and Poland until the early 17th century when the Counter-Reformation ended its existence. The church was revived a century later in Saxony, and the subsequent missionary zeal of the group brought the first Moravians to the New World in 1734.

The group that settled in North Carolina named

Single Brothers House: Old Salem, North Carolina. Open to the public.

their community Salem, inspired by the Hebrew word for "peace." These Germanic founders of Old Salem were a devout people who brought order, industry and education to their new home, and a special love for music, important in their services.

Unlike other American towns at that time, it was a planned community, and the buildings were constructed flush to the walks and clustered around a central square. By 1830, Salem had fulfilled its promise, becoming not only an important industrial center, but a cultural and educational oasis in the back country of southeast America.

The earliest major building still standing in the community is the Single Brothers House of 1768-1769. This home for unmarried men had as its first occupants 16 men and four boys who learned their trades there. Financially it was never a success, gradually losing money and occupants and fading into oblivion.

After 1823, the home became a boys' school and then an apartment house. In 1961 it was restored to its late 18th-century appearance and opened as a museum in November 1964.

The house now features the kitchen, dining room, chapel and nine craft shops. The shops where trades were once learned are today worked by a tinsmith, gunsmith, dyer, weaver, shoemaker, tailor, potter, joiner and cooper. In the dwelling's half-timber construction, the upright timbers of the framing are spaced two to three feet apart with diagonal bracing where needed. The interstices are filled with brick nogging, pargeted and whitewashed on the inside. The façade facing the square has three six-over-six-light windows evenly spaced across the two floors, and an overlighted entrance door. An amply proportioned gable roof is also one of the building's features.

Inside, the building has many of the characteristics of some of the other earlier houses: smooth whitewashed walls, handmade pavers and wide plank floors.

In the restoration of this building, its architectural potential has been realized to make it one of the most intriguing structures in America today — a segment of medieval Germanic Europe transferred to the Western Hemisphere.

Below: The Single Brothers House is the oldest major building extant in the 18th-century Moravian community at Old Salem. The planned community was named from the Hebrew word for peace and the house was a trade school for single men.

WILLIAM GIBBES HOUSE
HEYWARD-WASHINGTON HOUSE
CHARLESTON, SOUTH CAROLINA

Glittering Charleston

During the years immediately before and after the Revolution, Charleston, South Carolina, was one of the most remarkable cities in America. It was dominated by as exclusive and aristocratic a society as could be found in the colonies and the fledgling nation, a society that derived its wealth from two easily grown and sold crops — rice and indigo.

To escape the fumes and disease caused on the plantations by the annual flooding of the rice fields, the owners would spend several months a year in Charleston. The result was an illustrious oasis of civilization, about which Henry Adams said: "Nowhere in the Union [in 1800] was intelligence, wealth and education greater in proportion to numbers than in the little society of cotton and rice planters who ruled South Carolina."

Today, Charleston's 18th-century architecture is probably unequalled by any other city, as attested by two of its outstanding houses, the William Gibbes House and the Heyward-Washington House.

At the turn of the 18th century, Charleston was the site of an architecture craze. This was the time at which the English Adam style hit the Atlantic seaboard. In the Adam tradition, as modified and adapted in America, well-lighted rooms were arranged in suites varying in shape and proportion, with circular, oval, polygonal, rectangular or segmented ends. Classic proportions were given a sense of domestic scale. Walls and ceilings were covered with ornament in low relief, enclosing medallions of decorative painting, with gilding and clear, light colors which, along the Southern seaboard, perhaps helped to compensate for the depressing atmosphere outdoors during the rainy season. Rich and colorful materials were employed.

Above: Late in the 18th century, wealthy South Carolina planters spent the rainy season each year at Charleston while rice fields were flooded and disease ridden. The William Gibbes House was a typical product of this era.

William Gibbes House: 64 South Battery, Charleston, South Carolina. Private residence.
Heyward-Washington House: 87 Church Street, Charleston, South Carolina. Open to the public.

The William Gibbes House, built at the height of the Georgian period in Charleston, was extensively redecorated again in the midst of the craze for the Adam style. The result was both distinguished and pleasing.

The house was started soon after 1772 by William Gibbes, a typical, wealthy Charleston businessman-aristocrat. The Ashley River then came up to the opposite side of the street and Gibbes had a long wharf running out to the channel where he conducted business. In hot weather the wharf was used as a place of entertainment.

After its owner died, the house became the home of Mrs. Sarah Moore Smith and continued in her family. About 1800 the Smiths added the monumental marble stairways at the front, put a high cove to the parlor ceiling, and enriched much of the Georgian woodwork with Adam ornaments.

The Reverend John Grimke Drayton, who later owned the house, became the creator of the famous Magnolia Gardens, located several miles northwest of Charleston, after a "clergyman's throat" forced him from the active ministry.

In the 1920's Mrs. Washington A. Roebling, widow of the builder of the Brooklyn Bridge, bought the house from the Sloan family, whose home it had long been. Mrs. Roebling made extensive restoration and alterations. For her collection of Oriental art and ceramics the southeast room on the principal floor was remodeled in the mode of Chinese Chippendale. The rooms at the rear were lengthened and the brick stairway added to connect the house with the formal garden. It was the late 1920's that the beautiful walled garden at the Gibbes House was designed by the well-known landscape architect, Loutrel W. Briggs.

The Heyward-Washington House was built in 1770 by Daniel Heyward, prominent rice planter and father of Thomas Heyward, Jr.

Thomas Heyward, who lived in the house, was a delegate to the Continental Congress, signer of the Declaration of Independence for South Carolina and an early curator of the Charleston Museum.

The house is a characteristic Charleston "double-house," with a hall running through the center. It is entered from the street, with four rooms on each floor. The wood carving over the mantel in the drawing room is enhanced by the figure-eight design, carved in mahogany. There are doors entering into passageways next to the chimneys in all rooms. These were originally utilized either as closets or as "thoroughfare closets" leading into other rooms.

Behind the house are two buildings, the kitchen and Carriage House, which form a little courtyard. Beyond these buildings is a formal garden laid out in the 18th-century geometric pattern and planted with flowers in keeping with the period of the house. An English atmosphere and scene is presented as one looks out the window of the second floor onto the garden and brick buildings in the rear of the house.

Because of his participation in the determined defense of Charleston during the Revolutionary War, after the city fell to the British, Thomas Heyward was exiled, along with other prisoners, to Saint

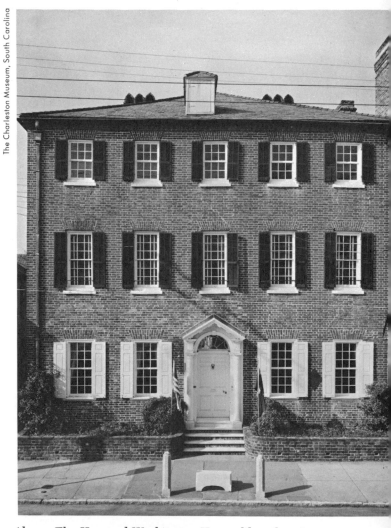

Above: The Heyward-Washington House, like others in Charleston, is an adaptation of the English Adam style which swept through the Southern colonies prior to the outbreak of the Revolutionary War. In 1791, George Washington leased the house from Thomas Heyward.

Augustine in 1780. During his exile, his wife and sister lived in the house. Mrs. Heyward defied a British order to illuminate her house in celebration of a military victory in 1781. During the uproar which followed her disobedience, her sister died. She was then exiled to Philadelphia and died there the following year.

One of the most important social events which took place at the Heyward-Washington House was George Washington's visit to the city in 1791 and his stay at the house. Washington leased the house from Thomas Heyward, Jr., who at that time was residing on his plantation near Ridgeland, South Carolina.

Today, the Heyward-Washington House is owned and administered by the Charleston Museum, and has been redecorated and refurnished with outstanding Charleston-made furniture.

GUNSTON HALL

LORTON, VIRGINIA

Memorial to Greatness

Gunston Hall, like its builder, George Mason, is typical of a great period in the history of Virginia and of the nation. In the late 18th century, Virginia contributed to American history such men as Washington, Jefferson, Madison, Monroe, Patrick Henry, the Lees, the Randolphs and George Mason. Mason was the author of the Fairfax Resolves, written in 1774, summarizing the grievances of the American Colonies against the mother country. In 1776 he took the lead in writing the "Declaration of Rights," part of the first Virginia Constitution. In December 1701, the Federal Bill of Rights, based upon Mason's "Declaration of Rights," became law. In addition, George Mason wrote, with James Madison, the oath administered to the President at his inauguration. It is not difficult to understand why Mason was sometimes called the "Pen of the Revolution."

Mason began building his home in 1755, and in 1758 he and his wife moved into Gunston Hall, which they named for an ancestral home in Staffordshire, England. Mason brought William Buckland, a young carpenter and joiner, from England to complete the house. Appearing quite simple from the outside, a story-and-a-half square brick house, its steep roof accented by pairs of tall chimneys at each end, Gunston's interiors are among the most impressive of the colonial period. The splendidly carved woodwork of the Palladian drawing room is,

perhaps, unequalled in America.

The furnishing of Gunston Hall has been accomplished through gifts of original Mason items, the purchase of others and the acquisition of furniture and objects made before George Mason's death in 1792. The philosophy of the furnishings has been defined by the fact that Mason wrote the Non-Importation Regulations in 1769; therefore, no English furniture made after that date has been used.

Of particular note is the dining room at Gunston Hall. Furnished in antique Chinese Chippendale, it is reputed to be the first colonial arrangement based on Oriental designs. Already fashionable in London, William Buckland introduced the Eastern style into the colonies when he arrived from England to complete the work on Gunston Hall.

The 18th-century gardens which George Mason planted had disappeared by 1912, but the great box hedges mostly remained. The gardens were replaced under the guidance of a written description of them left by John Mason (1766-1849). In 1949, the Garden Club of Virginia undertook the restoration of the gardens to an 18th-century pattern. Features unknown to Virginia gardens in George Mason's time, including the 19th-century garden ornaments and two pools, were removed. The Garden Club also replanted all beds with flowers and shrubs

Gunston Hall: Route 242, Lorton, Virginia. Open to the public.

Above: Called the "Pen of the American Revolution," George Mason completed Gunston Hall in 1758. His 1776 Virginia "Declaration of Rights" was the basis for the later Federal Bill of Rights. He also co-authored the Presidential oath of office.

known in the 18th century.

Gunston Hall stands today as a memorial to George Mason and to the principles of just government and civic righteousness. His "Virginia Declaration of Rights" opens with these words: "All men are by nature equally free and independent." It encompasses the principles of personal rights without which independence would be a mockery — freedom of religion and the press, and freedom from unjust trial and punishment.

In his adherence to individual rights George Mason stood firm to the end. He refused to support the Constitution because at first it had no Bill of Rights. He was bitter that the new Republic did not at once outlaw the slave trade. He saw clearly the new horizons that lay beyond the frontier and was chiefly responsible for sending young George Rogers Clark to explore the Northwest Territory.

JOHN MARSHALL HOUSE
RICHMOND, VIRGINIA

"The Personification of Justice"

When John Marshall died the Liberty Bell in Philadelphia was tolled — and cracked. Much honored in his time, this statesman of our country's Federal Era is remembered today as the greatest Chief Justice and as a scholar, soldier, citizen, diplomat and patriot.

John Marshall was born in Fauquier County, Virginia, in 1755, the eldest of 15 children of Colonel Thomas Marshall and his wife, Mary Randolph Keith. Through the Randolph family and by his marriage to Mary Willis Ambler, he was related to many of Virginia's leading political figures, including Thomas Jefferson, "Light Horse" Harry Lee, Edmund Randolph and John Randolph of Roanoke, noted statesmen who were his contemporaries.

Marshall grew up at "Oakhill," a comfortable seven-room house on his father's estate overlooking the Valley of Virginia. His home was superior to most frontier homes of that day and place. He had the guidance of educated parents and of a capable tutor, Reverend James Thompson. When 14 years of age, he was sent to Westmoreland County to The Classical Academy where his father and George Washington had been students and friends and where James Monroe was his schoolmate.

As a young man, Marshall served as captain in the Revolutionary War. He studied law at the College of William and Mary under the famous George Wythe and was elected to the Phi Beta Kappa Society while there. This historic college now has named its law school "The Marshall-Wythe School of Law." Marshall was admitted to the Bar in 1780 and soon became politically active. He was a strong Federalist. To use his own words, he was "convinced that no safe or permanent remedy could be found but in a more efficient and better organized general government."

He was elected to the Virginia Assembly in 1782 and in the same year was appointed a member of the Council of the State of Virginia. In 1787 he took a leading part in the Virginia Convention called to determine state action on the proposed United States Constitution. He declined appointment in 1796 as Attorney General of the United States. The following year he was sent as envoy extraordinary to France by President Adams. He was elected to Congress in 1799, and in 1800 President Adams appointed him Secretary of State. Marshall was appointed Chief Justice of the United States Supreme Court in 1801, an office he held until his death in 1835. As one of the nation's greatest jurists, he contributed immeasurably to the sound interpretation of the Constitution.

John Marshall's house is a perfect example of a late 18th-century gentleman's town residence. Designed by Marshall and completed in 1790, it served as his home until his death. Architecturally the house represents a transition between the Georg-

John Marshall House: 818 Marshall Street, Richmond, Virginia. Open to the public.

ian and Federal periods. Characteristic of its creator, sturdy and dignified, the house contains simple lines and refined ornamentation. It is furnished with fine antiques of the period, including many Marshall pieces. The house contains an interesting collection of his books, china and glass.

After Marshall's death, the house remained in his family until 1909 when sold to the City of Richmond. Later the city placed the house in the custody of the Association for the Preservation of Virginia Antiquities to preserve this historic house as a memorial to John Marshall. The house was formally opened to the public in 1913.

John Marshall's home is one of Richmond's most important houses. It is a shrine to the memory of one of the nation's most famous statesmen and jurists during the formative years of the Republic. In the words of Judge Joseph Story, his associate on the bench, "he seemed the very personification of Justice itself as he administered at its altars in the presence of the Nation."

Below: Portrait of Chief Justice Marshall hangs in the Marshall dining room. Cabinet holds china and waterford glass used by the Marshalls at the turn of the 18th century. Noted relatives of Marshall included the Lees, Randolphs and Jeffersons.

JOSEPH VANN HOUSE
CHATSWORTH, GEORGIA

A Cherokee Rose

Clement Vann, a Scottish trader, settled among the Cherokee Indians early in the 18th century. He married a Cherokee woman who bore him several children. One was James Vann, builder of the Vann House. When Moravian missionaries came to the area, Vann gave them land and helped them build their houses. The Moravians recorded that Vann was generous when sober but pugnacious when under the influence of liquor.

James Vann wished to leave his vast holdings to his son, Joseph, but the Council of Chiefs intervened to divide the property equally between his widow and all of his children. Nevertheless, Joe Vann acquired the Vann House and most of the property given to him and his mother. He was an even better businessman than his father and soon became known as "Rich Joe" Vann by whites and Indians alike.

The Vann House was the showplace of the Cherokee nation in the early 1800's. The house, completed in 1804, is an outstanding example of Moravian workmanship in the Federal style of architecture. The solid brick walls are laid in both Flemish and English bonds from bricks made on the place. The handwrought nails and hinges were produced in James Vann's own blacksmith shops. Hand carving, with the Cherokee Rose predominating, is both inside and outside the building.

On each of the two main floors there are two rooms, 30-by-20 feet, with a wide hallway between. To the left of the main entrance an elaborately carved staircase is the oldest example of balanced or cantilevered construction in Georgia. The room to the right of the entrance on the first floor was the parlor with a huge open fireplace surmounted by a mantel reaching the high ceiling. Under many layers of paint and grime on the carved mantel and wainscoting, the original decoration was blue, red, green and yellow, the colors of nature in north Georgia — blue sky, red clay soil, green trees, and yellow, ripened grain. These colors prevail all over the house.

At the time of the Cherokee Removal, the Federal Government paid Joseph Vann $19,605 for his brick house, 800 acres of cultivated land, 42 cabins, six barns, five smokehouses, a grist mill, blacksmith shop, eight corn cribs, a shop and foundry, a trading post, peach kiln, a still, 1,133 peach trees, 147 apple trees and other property.

Turned out of their home on a cold day in March 1834, Joe Vann and his family made their

Phil McCafferty

Above: When President Andrew Jackson enforced the Indian removal from Eastern lands in 1834, Cherokee Joseph Vann surrendered his home, 65 accompanying buildings and 800 acres of cultivated land to the Federal Government for $19,605.

Joseph Vann House: U.S. Route 76, Chatsworth, Georgia. Open to the public.

way to a farm he owned in Tennessee. Later, they traveled to Weber Falls, Oklahoma, where he built a duplicate of the Vann House in Georgia.

The Vann House deteriorated for 100 years despite the protests of national historians. Finally in 1952, an aroused community purchased the house and three acres of land and gave them to the Georgia Historical Commission. The roof was gone; the dining room floor had collapsed; the brick arches over the doors had cracked and were falling in; and every windowpane was shattered by vandals.

Over a period of several years the Georgia Historical Commission restored the building and partially furnished it. The commission received assistance from the Whitfield-Murray County Historical Society, and Scalamandre, Inc., of New York gave the material for the elaborate period draperies. The house was dedicated in July 1958, before a distinguished gathering of leaders of the Cherokees, 42 descendants of the Vann family and interested Georgians. Many priceless relics of the family were returned to the house as exhibits.

ASHLAND
LEXINGTON, KENTUCKY

"Friend and Favorite"

Ashland is one of America's most famous houses. For 40 years it was the residence of Henry Clay, a distinguished lawyer and one of the nation's great masters of statecraft.

Henry Clay purchased the land on which he built his home in 1805. According to tradition, it was designed by the renowned architect, Benjamin Latrobe, who supervised completion of the United States Capitol in Washington and designed the exterior porticoes of the White House. The park or lawn about the home and the walks were probably laid out by Pierre Charles L'Enfant, the famous French landscape architect, who helped George Washington lay out the nation's capital city.

Clay christened the home Ashland because it was located in a forest of majestic ash trees. It is said that Clay wrote many of his Congressional speeches while he walked through the grove of ash, and the wood of many of these trees was used for the finished wood interior of the home.

The house itself was typical of the large plantation homes of the South and, in its architectural design, seemed to summon into prominence the lavish mansions of the ante-bellum period. A solid, brick central unit, flanked by two smaller wings, is capped by a short, sloping roof with elaborate

cornice work, which terminates in gabled pediments. A modest projection from the center of the roof is also pedimented and overlooks the wrought-iron balustrade of a second-story balcony. Below this, pilastered doric columns adorn the front portico.

Reflecting the expansiveness of Clay's career, the ivy-covered mansion sits in the shade of a Ginko tree, believed to be one of the oldest of its kind in America, which was presented to Clay by the Japanese government. The interior of the house, also, is a record of his travels and his work. China imported from France adorns the Clay dining room, and an Italian Carrara marble mantel around the parlor fireplace is carved to depict the four seasons. Draperies, also purchased in France, were brought back by Clay in 1814, after signing the Treaty of Ghent which concluded the War of 1812; and in 1844, when Clay aspired to the Presidency for the last time, the Whig ladies of Philadelphia presented him with a quilt which is on display in one of the upper bed chambers.

Henry Clay was not only a lawyer and statesman, but also a good farmer and stock breeder. He loved the soil and was interested in the substance it might yield for the welfare of mankind. He imported expensive stock from Spain, France and

Ashland: East Main Street & Sycamore Rd., Lexington, Kentucky. Open to the public. Color illustration, p. 106

England and was known among his associates as a great lover of sports.

The kind of a man Henry Clay was is aptly expressed in this portion of a speech delivered by Judge Samuel Wilson at the presentation of the Henry Clay statue in 1930 at Frankfort, Kentucky: "The life of this great man is a part, an important and inseparable part, of the life of his country. If Washington was the Father of his Country, Henry Clay was emphatically the faithful Friend and prime Favorite of his countrymen; and like Washington and Lincoln . . . he belongs to the ages."

Among Henry Clay's accomplishments were the roles he played in promoting internal improvements, in re-establishing the Bank of the United States and thus stabilizing the currency and facilitating exchange, in strengthening and popularizing a protective tariff, in reinvigorating the Navy and encouraging our Merchant Marine, in favoring emancipation of the slaves and in rendering service toward the preservation of the Union. The entire national banking system of this country owes its existence to Henry Clay. Peace in the Western world between independent nations was rendered possible by the bold concept of "Pan-Americanism" of which Henry Clay was the author.

Today, a new and recent honor has come to Clay. The members of the United States Senate decided to have the portraits of the five most distinguished and most influential Senators painted and hung in the Cloak Room just off the Senate floor. Henry Clay's portrait hangs in the central position of this group.

MONTICELLO

CHARLOTTESVILLE, VIRGINIA

Thomas Jefferson: Many-Sided Genius

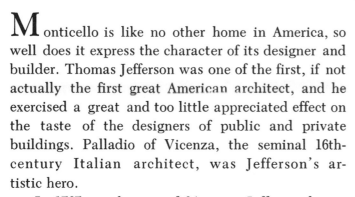

Monticello is like no other home in America, so well does it express the character of its designer and builder. Thomas Jefferson was one of the first, if not actually the first great American architect, and he exercised a great and too little appreciated effect on the taste of the designers of public and private buildings. Palladio of Vicenza, the seminal 16th-century Italian architect, was Jefferson's artistic hero.

In 1767, at the age of 24 years, Jefferson began making plans for his house. The Monticello plantation that Jefferson erected was unique. It was built, unlike any previous one, on a leveled plateau on the top of a mountain 857 feet above sea level. To make all parts of the mountain accessible, Jefferson constructed on its slopes at four different levels, paths or, as he called them, roundabouts. They were connected by oblique roads.

Leveling of the hilltop began in 1768, construction of the main house several years later. By 1782, the first version of Monticello had been completed. Remodeling began about 1793 and was not finished until after 1809, when the second, or present-day Monticello, assumed its familiar form.

Before Jefferson built Monticello, there was on every plantation a series of small outbuildings such as the laundry, smoke house, sometimes a schoolhouse and always a kitchen. These Jefferson sought to render inconspicuous by locating them beneath the long terrace walks terminating in the two balanced out-chambers. Connecting these terraces is the all-weather passageway in which are placed the wine room, beer cellar, cider room and rum cellar. Beneath the south terrace are to be found the kitchen, the cook's room, servants' room, smoke room and the dairy. The small pavilion on the end of this terrace is on the site of the first dwelling to be erected on the mountain top. It was completed in time for Jefferson to bring his bride, Martha Wayles Skelton, to it in 1772, thus giving basis for the name

Monticello: Charlottesville, Virginia. Open to the public. Color illustration, p. 106.

"Honeymoon Cottage."

The house is one of the classic examples of American architecture. It is a three-story building of 35 rooms including 12 in the basement. The dominating feature is the dome which commands the garden or west front. The dome was the first erected over an American house. The room under the dome, octagonal in shape, is often referred to as the ballroom; however Jefferson always referred to it as the sky or dome room.

The absence of any important staircase in the main hall is often commented upon. In the extensive remodeling which began in 1793, Jefferson, in the interest of economy and space and probably privacy, constructed in each wing very narrow (24 inches wide), steep and winding staircases. These extend from the basement floor to the third or top floor.

The gardens on the east and west lawns of Monticello, neglected for many years, were restored in 1939 and 1940 according to Jefferson's plans. Several drawings were found among his papers showing the scheme he projected and ultimately executed. On one is indicated the long gravel walk with its borders that circumscribes the west lawn, as well as the semi-circle of shrubs and trees in front of the house. Another shows the arrangement of the oval and circular beds near the house which Jefferson himself laid out in 1807. The plants for each bed are listed in his garden and farm books and the directions were carefully followed in the restoration. Near the pavilion that terminates the south terrace is the fish pond that Jefferson kept well stocked with fish caught in nearby streams. Thus, today, one may see

Jefferson's Monticello much as it was when he retired to enjoy the last years of his life there among his family and gardens.

Jefferson died at Monticello at the age of 83 on July 4, 1826. Monticello was sold five years later to James T. Barclay who retained possession until 1836 when he sold the property to Uriam P. Levy, an admirer of Jefferson and an officer in the United States Navy. The Levy period of ownership of 87 years was considerably longer than that of Jefferson or his descendants. In 1923 the house and about 683 acres was purchased by the Thomas Jefferson Memorial Foundation.

The foundation purchased the plantation, which now consists of 700 acres, for $500,000. The foundation's purpose is to preserve the house and restore the gardens as they were in Jefferson's day. In 1954 $250,000 was spent renovating the house, including the installation of a heating system of remote heat control, an air conditioning unit, and other modernizing devices. Other improvements on the house and gardens have brought the capital outlay expenditure to well over $750,000.

Monticello, the home of Thomas Jefferson, remains a symbol of a man who served his country in a superior way as drafter of the Declaration of Independence, Governor of Virginia, Secretary of State under Washington, Vice-President of the United States under John Adams, and as the third American President, an aristocratic man with humanitarian and intellectual interests — a rare figure in any society.

JAMES KNOX POLK HOME
COLUMBIA, TENNESSEE

"Napoleon of the Stump"

Samuel Polk, father of the President, with his wife and children, crossed the mountains of North Carolina in 1806 to the new State of Tennessee and settled in the picturesque region of Duck River. Ten years later he bought the tract of land and built the home destined to become a national shrine.

James Knox Polk was the oldest of ten children.

His father was an enterprising farmer, his mother a devout Presbyterian who was to outlive her son. Polk was eleven years old when his father moved the family from North Carolina to middle Tennessee.

Polk entered the University of North Carolina in 1815, and four years later began the study of law at Nashville under the distinguished guidance of

James Knox Polk Home: West Seventh Street, Columbia, Tennessee. Open to the public.

Above: The spacious main entrance of Monticello reveals Thomas Jefferson's love of classical beauty. His inventive genius, too, is apparent in the seven-day clock over the entrance way. Operated by weighted pulleys, the calendar indicates each day of the week. Below: The ancestral home of James Knox Polk is representative of the period and locality.

Judge Felix Grundy. After practicing law in Columbia, Tennessee, the future President was elected to the Legislature of Tennessee in 1883, and from then on he enjoyed a successful political career which did not end until he retired after serving four years as President of the United States.

In 1825, while in the legislature, Polk was elected to Congress where he championed the cause of Andrew Jackson and Martin Van Buren. He soon became leader of the Democratic forces in the historical struggle against the Whigs, which finally resulted in the annihilation of that once powerful party. He was the leader in Congress upon whom Jackson relied for the passage of administrative bills.

Polk was elected Speaker of the House in 1835 and was re-elected Speaker of the next, or 25th, Congress. He was firm but calm throughout the sessions over which he presided, which were turbulent and exciting because of the slavery issue which was seriously beginning to divide the Union. After his service as Speaker at Washington, he ran for the office of Governor of Tennessee and, because of his great personal popularity, won, defeating the Whigs who were in the majority.

In 1844 Polk was nominated for President at the Democratic Convention in Baltimore. He has been called the first "dark-horse" candidate in American politics, for he made no active campaign and was nominated unanimously.

"Who is James K. Polk?" the Whigs chanted derisively during the hotly contested Presidential campaign. They said he was an obscure, mediocre man who was not big enough to become President. However, Polk was swept into office, probably because the voters agreed with his urging that the United States annex Texas, California and Oregon. He was the youngest President elected before 1845.

Sometimes called "Young Hickory" because of his admiration of and similarity to Andrew Jackson, he was also called "The Napoleon of the Stump" because he was such a stirring orator. The only strong President between Jackson and Lincoln, Polk governed with a determined will and intense energy that probably led to his early death at 54, just three months after he left the Presidency.

The commotion which preceded the Civil War, almost immediately obscured his administration's major accomplishments, but they have seldom been excelled. He secured the annexation of Texas, Oregon and California and New Mexico; he stabilized the internal policy of the United States (opposing "pork barrel" legislation, refusing to spend public funds); he forced Great Britain to conclude a treaty giving America equal and reciprocal rights on the high seas, on mail rates and other matters; and he founded the United States Naval Academy.

In recent years, a re-evaluation of his greatness has begun to be made, and his stature is constantly increasing. In 1938, a commission of 55 outstanding authorities on American history were invited by Arthur M. Schlesinger to appraise and rate the Presidents. This commission placed James K. Polk along with Theodore Roosevelt, Grover Cleveland and John Adams as one of the "near-great" Presidents, preceded only by six "great" Presidents.

The ancestral home of James Knox Polk, typical of its locality and period, is of handmade brick. The architect is not known and may have been Samuel Polk himself. The Holland method of bricklaying is used on the west side of the building, while the usual type is employed elsewhere. The front door is typically colonial with fan shaped transom.

Downstairs the doors are of white ash, while yellow poplar is used upstairs. With the exception of the study, original mantels are still standing; the window frames and sash are handmade.

From Samuel Polk's will and court records, it is deduced that he was a prosperous farmer, surveyor and landowner. The same records indicate that the ancestral estate had a flower garden, kitchen garden and the usual auxiliary structures.

The house today contains much memorabilia of the President and his handsome wife Sarah, such as her inaugural fan. In the double-parlor is a round, marble mosaic table of the President's, with a large American eagle on top bearing the motto of the United States and surrounded by a circle of 30 stars — a reminder that 552,568 square miles were added to the United States during the administration of James K. Polk, enabling it to become a truly continent-spanning power.

ARLINGTON
D'EVEREUX
STANTON HALL
NATCHEZ, MISSISSIPPI

When Cotton Was King

On a high bluff on the eastern bank of the Mississippi River, Fort Rosalie was established in July 1716, in the name of Louis XIV, the "Sun King" of France. This is the present-day site of Natchez, Mississippi, the oldest city on the great river. Later passing through British and Spanish hands, the American flag was first raised there in 1798.

Shortly after the turn of the century, Natchez and the entire South began its half-century of wealth and splendor — the legendary golden age when cotton was king. The first steamboat came to Natchez in 1811, and within a decade the combination of cotton and steam had made it one of the wealthiest towns in America.

Nothing conveys the opulence of this era better than the grand houses built by the owners of the cotton plantations. At one time, within 200 miles of New Orleans, many of these magnificent dwellings could be seen within sight of each other on both sides of the river. Today, Natchez, with the finest collection of ante-bellum mansions in the South, comes the nearest to reflecting the glory of those former days; and three houses — Arlington, D'Evereux and Stanton Hall, built between 1816 and 1851 — give an excellent summary of the period and the houses it produced.

Arlington, with its high ceilings, is one of the best examples of Georgian architecture in the South and one · of the most distinguished houses along the Mississippi River. Built in 1816 by Jane Surget White, Arlington still contains its original furnishings.

The death of Mrs. White the day following a ball given in honor of the opening of the home is supposed to have been mysterious. But Mrs. Anne Vaughan, the present owner, discounts the tale.

Arlington is a massive, red-brick structure situated on a 75-acre area of land, like an island in the heart of Natchez, a step from Main Street. It is fronted by a double gallery upheld by four stately Doric columns. In many of the Natchez houses, the brick was made on the grounds by slaves; but the brick for Arlington was imported from England. Every window and outside door has a facing of white marble, accenting the white-marble entrance steps and portico. All four of the main doorways are noteworthy. Tremendous fan lights and side lights are exquisitely designed.

Downstairs is a large hall, which is 17½ feet in height, with two rooms on either side. The pleasant music room contains a crystal chandelier, family portraits and a harp. In the dining room, silver by Tallois of Paris, rare china and crystal may be seen. Upholstery and hangings of satin damask suggest the name "Gold Drawing Room" for the parlor. This room is decorated with century-old curtains caught with tie-backs of white grapes against gilt-bronze grape leaves. Refined rendering of detail makes the cornices, gold leaf mirrors, carved lintels and finely cut interior trim impressive.

In the sunroom at the rear of the house is assembled one of the most interesting collections of antique dolls, nearly a thousand of them, as well as

---

Arlington: East Main Street, Natchez, Mississippi. Open to the public (March 4-April 2).

D'Evereux: U.S. Route 61 North, Natchez, Mississippi. Open to the public (March 4-April 2). Color illustration, p. 103.

Stanton Hall: High Street, Natchez, Mississippi. Open to the public.

Above: Arlington, like other plantation homes in the deep South prior to the Civil War, reflected the vast cotton fortunes that were so closely linked to the institution of slavery. All the brick for its construction was imported from England.

an antique doll house. Among collections of china, books, silver and furniture is a glass collection.

On the grounds of Arlington is some of the oldest and finest shrubbery in Natchez. There is a row of pale pink azaleas that a former owner brought from China many years ago. Since then, that variety has been propagated throughout Natchez. Among the camellia bushes on the estate is one thought to be the tallest of its kind in the country. It rises above a second-story window sill.

The D'Evereux mansion is an example of a pure classic type of Southern colonial architecture reminiscent of a Greek temple. D'Evereux fulfills the traditional concept of Southern architecture and for years has been a leading attraction in Natchez.

The splendid white structure has a spacious front gallery supported by six lofty, fluted Doric columns. The large, recessed doorway is overhung by a lacy wrought-iron balcony. Surmounting the whole is an observation tower or cupola with a bannistered widow's walk.

Inside, at the end of the wide, spacious hall, a doorway framed with fanshaped lights and sidelights of lacy design, offers a sharp contrast to the severe lines of the front door lights. Handsomely furnished in antiques are the double drawing room

SOUTHERN HOUSES

Left: The Royal Coat of Arms of King George III appears at the front of Tryon Palace. Made of carved and emblazoned mahogany, the escutcheon of the House of Hanover is the central feature. The two mottos read, "Shame be to him who evil thinks" and "God and my right."

Tryon Palace Commission

Above: Delicate wrought-iron gates and railing mark the approach to the Tryon Palace in New Bern, North Carolina. The unique English-style home, begun in 1767, became the first fixed colonial capitol of the state in 1770 and also served as the governor's residence.

Above: The Custis-Lee Mansion in Arlington, Virginia, is distinctive through its long association with families of historical prominence. It was from this home that Colonel and Mrs. Robert E. Lee left for Richmond following news of the secession of Virginia in April 1861.

*Above: The Lee Mansion, noted for its hospitality,
was rarely without guests who were often entertained
in the handsome family dining room. According to legend,
it was here that Lee proposed marriage to Mary Custis
while she was cutting him a piece of fruitcake.*

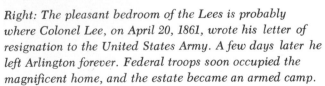

*Right: The pleasant bedroom of the Lees is probably
where Colonel Lee, on April 20, 1861, wrote his letter of
resignation to the United States Army. A few days later he
left Arlington forever. Federal troops soon occupied the
magnificent home, and the estate became an armed camp.*

Adam Thoroughgood House

Below: The mellowed Adam Thoroughgood House in Virginia Beach, Virginia, built by an early English settler, was constructed from bricks made and dried on the site. Left: Fine pewter and colorful waxed fruit form a still-life arrangement in the charming home.

FPG by Taylor Lewis

(Continued from page 122)

on the right and dining room on the left. In the stairwell, a graceful, semi-circular stairway guarded by mahogany rails mounts to the third floor.

D'Evereux mansion was built in 1840 by William St. John Elliot and was under construction almost four years. The land on which it stands was purchased in 1836. The architect who designed D'Evereux was James Hardy, a long-time associate of Levi G. Weeks, whom government historians concede was the originator of the classic architecture of Natchez. Little is known of Hardy, but to him and Weeks, more than to any other individuals, Natchez owes credit for its architectural tradition.

When D'Evereux was completed, the Elliots decided to name it in honor of Mr. Elliot's distinguished maternal uncle, General John D'Evereux, an international hero of that era, who won fame as an aide and close companion of Simón Bolívar, the liberator of five South American countries.

Elliot was a personal friend and strong advocate of Henry Clay and frequently entertained him on his various campaign travels. Clay recorded his pleasant memories of D'Evereux in the *Congressional Record*.

D'Evereux was sold in the 1930's to Miss Myra Virginia Smith, a retired teacher and civic worker. As a graduate of the University of Chicago, such was her loyalty to the school that she willed most of her real estate to the institution with the understanding that funds derived therefrom be used to found scholarships for deserving students. In June 1962, D'Evereux was sold to the T. B. Buckles family of Natchez. They have preserved the noted landmark and have also completed a restoration of the entire building.

Stanton Hall is recognized as one of the most palatial and imposing ante-bellum houses in the South. It was a fitting culmination to the period of lavish living in Natchez in the decades before the Civil War.

Stanton Hall was planned and built by Robert Rose for Frederick Stanton, a wealthy Natchez merchant. Rose and Stanton went to Europe for the purpose of chartering a ship to bring to Natchez the materials and furniture to be used to construct and furnish Stanton Hall. It is believed that Rose, who also built another fine Natchez home, Melrose, selected most of the furnishings, including the enormous gold-leaf mirrors and bronze chandeliers of unusual designs representing eras of Natchez history.

Stanton spared no expense in making this the most beautiful house in Natchez. While the bricks for the building were being burned by slaves and the walls were taking shape in Natchez, his chartered ship brought home workmen, as well as the mirrors, chandeliers and other expensive items, such as the Carrara marble mantels.

Today a city block forms the grounds for Stanton Hall. A heavy iron grill fence surrounds it. In later years this beautiful house is said to have been sold for less than the cost of the fence.

The house has large double galleries, supported by towering Grecian columns. Both upper and lower galleries are enclosed by beautifully designed wrought-iron grill rails of roses. The floor of the upper gallery is of gray and white marble and the wide steps are granite. Fluted columns frame the massive entrance door. The building has a tremendous hall on its lower floor, 74 feet long, which runs between four large rooms. Suspended midway in the hall is a carved ceiling arch covered in Oriental design. The same motif is displayed in doorways entering the other rooms and in the carved interior woodwork throughout the floor.

The large rooms of the house create a feeling of spaciousness. The immense ballroom, 72 feet long, contains mirrors at opposite ends, which make endless reflections of the chandelier lights between them. Across the hall is the library with mantels carved of Carrara marble, a large mirror and a chandelier. Beyond, a recessed stair with mahogany rails leads upward in elliptical loops past six bedrooms to the attic floor. In the great dining room, vast dimensions are complemented with twin fireplaces and twin chandeliers.

The builder of Stanton Hall died suddenly a few months after he moved into the house. Then came the Civil War, and in the years that followed, the elegant house changed hands several times. In 1940 the Pilgrimage Garden Club purchased the house and has restored it to its former brilliance. In fact, today this most elaborate of all Natchez houses is probably more beautiful than ever because the live oaks that were saplings in Stanton's day are tall and majestic.

Above: Stanton Hall, appearing like a fantasy through the lace of surrounding trees, passed through several owners following the Civil War. At one time it sold for less than the cost of the wrought-iron fence which encompasses the estate.

OWENS-THOMAS HOUSE
SAVANNAH, GEORGIA

Famous Architect's Beginning

The Owens-Thomas House has been called by competent critics one of the finest American examples of the English Regency period, a Greco-Roman architectural phase of the Classic Revival.

William Jay, talented young English architect, designed the house in England, for Richard Richardson, a prosperous Savannah merchant. It was begun in 1816 and finished in 1819. Richardson lost the house in the depression that began in 1820, and later the Bank of the United States took it over, selling it in 1830 to George Welchman Owens, whose descendants occupied the house for 121 years. It was the home of Owens' granddaughter, Margaret Gray Thomas. At her death in 1951, it became the property of the Telfair Academy of Arts and Sciences, Inc. to be maintained as a museum under the terms of her will. The house was opened to the public in 1954.

With the Owens-Thomas House as a beginning, William Jay attained a place of distinction among the great architects who have worked in this country. Jay was only 21 years old when he arrived in Savannah to supervise the building of the house. He was gay, witty and charming — the son of one of England's most famous non-conformist clergymen, the Reverend William Jay, and Anne Davis, daughter of a Church of England minister.

When Jay was born, the Classic Revival, set off by the discovery of ancient remains, was in its heyday. The excavation of Pompeii, first uncovered in 1762, especially inspired the whole civilized world.

In America, where architects of ability were still scarce, George Washington and Thomas Jefferson became leaders of the new classicism. The capitol at Richmond was designed by Jefferson after a study of French buildings of Roman inspiration. It is cited as the first building in the form of a temple in America, the beginning of the Federal style.

William Jay was sent to London as an apprentice to an architect when his talents were discovered. It was about this time that Thomas Bruce brought to London the famous Elgin Marbles dug from the soil of Athens in 1801.

The English Regency style is best described as a

Above: Vertical masonry scrolls serve as decorative supports to the south balcony of the Owens-Thomas House. It was from this balcony that the Marquis de Lafayette addressed the people of Savannah during a visit in 1825.

Owens-Thomas House Museum: 124 Abercorn Street, Savannah, Georgia. Open to the public.

"restrained Greco-Roman classicism." Its aim was to reveal beautiful classical lines. Interiors were designed to show off furniture especially made to reveal such lines. Walls were stripped of mass-decoration where motif was obscured in an elaboration of detail. Decoration was used only to break the monotony or to change the effect of shape. This last use is exemplified in the ceiling of the salon of the Owens-Thomas House in which two Greek fret circles with fluted spandrels descend slightly, like drapery, to create an expansive room.

The Owens-Thomas House abounds in examples of the way designs can be used to achieve their most dramatic effect. As one enters the dining room, the first thing that catches the eye is the Greek Key design. Set in a niche, high on the wall, a narrow, horizontal window of amber glass throws the Key into dramatic relief, and brings the northern light into the room so that it looks like direct sunlight.

Jay built other houses, such as the Telfair Mansion housing the Telfair Academy, and the Wayne-Gordon House, birthplace of Juliette Gordon Low, founder of the Girl Scouts of America, which still stands. Several other Jay houses of distinction have been demolished through the years.

Jay's difficulties were great. He had to deal with unknown workmen and unfamiliar materials. Many materials had to be imported; for example the bog-oak of the hall stairs of the Owens-Thomas House came from Ireland.

After 1824, when Jay returned to England, his inspiration failed, and his years there were un-productive. Later he went out to the Island of Mauritius in the Indian Ocean to build public buildings. The English Regency period was probably also in a sense the period of William Jay — the one best suited to his talents. It was giving way to the Greek Revival when Jay died at the young age of 32 on Mauritius.

Below: English Architect William Jay designed the Owens-Thomas House in what was known as the English Regency style, adapted from classical structures. The salon is furnished primarily with Duncan Phyfe, Allison and Sheraton pieces.

Above: The White House of the Confederacy was the Confederate Presidential home of Jefferson Davis during most of the Civil War. The rear garden is an imitation, but the two flanking horse chestnut trees are of mid-19th-century vintage.

THE WHITE HOUSE OF THE CONFEDERACY
RICHMOND, VIRGINIA

Leader of a Lost Cause

Jefferson Davis is one of the most tragic figures in American history; but, although he is still somewhat controversial, there is virtually no disagreement today as to whether or not he was the one best fitted for the position of President of the Confederacy. As Professor Kenneth Stampp of the University of California declared in 1955: "Those who contend that the South made a mistake by elevating Davis to the Presidency of the Confederacy have not yet come up with a man who would have done a better job in that difficult position."

The Confederate President could never be swerved from the theme that conscience and moral law should govern all his political decisions. Once in the United States Senate he had said impulsively, "What my heart tells me is right, nothing can prevail upon me not to do."

Good sense, however, was fundamental in Davis' make-up. This good sense revealed itself in his judgment, his taste, and in a rare acumen of practical affairs. It was interwoven with an extraordinary sensitivity, and his sensitivity had its counterpart in his deep humanity. While he lacked the ruthlessness that generally dominates revolutionary leaders, Davis possessed real military gifts and a remarkable insight into war strategy.

Born in a log cabin in Kentucky in 1808, Davis was named for Thomas Jefferson, whom Davis' father greatly admired. He graduated from West Point and fought with bravery in the Black Hawk War in Wisconsin. There he fell in love with Sarah Knox, daughter of Colonel Zachary Taylor, who was

The White House of the Confederacy, Confederate Museum: 1201 East Clay St., Richmond, Virginia. Open to the public.

later to be President of the United States. He resigned his commission in 1835 to marry her, but she died in Mississippi of malarial fever a few weeks after the wedding. He was so grief stricken that be became something of a recluse for seven years, but was remarried — to Varina Howell of Natchez — in 1845, the same year he was elected to the United States Congress.

He resigned his seat in 1846 to become a colonel in the Mexican War. Returning as a hero, he was appointed to a vacancy in the Senate. In 1853 President Franklin Pierce made him his Secretary of War, a position in which he earned an unsurpassed reputation. After the death in 1850 of John C. Calhoun, Davis became the foremost Southerner in politics. When the Southern states seceded in 1860 and 1861 he reluctantly went along with them.

When be became President of the Confederacy

in 1861, the infant republic lacked arms and equipment and was in a generally poor state of affairs. How he met this chaotic state is a matter of history. Davis regarded honorable defeat as only less glorious than victory. To give up while there was

Above: Jefferson Davis' gloves lay on a table beside an 1863 guide to Virginia in the master bedroom of the White House of the Confederacy. Below: Italian mantelpiece, depicting Cupid and Psyche, was installed in the parlor by Dr. John Brockenbrough in 1820. Only pieces of drapes and cornices remain after the Union invasion of Virginia.

the possibility of success would have been treasonous and would have ended the struggle without honor.

An angular white-stuccoed brick house in Richmond, now known as "The White House of the Confederacy," was the home of Jefferson Davis and his family during the years he served as President of the Confederacy. The house, designed by Robert Mills, was begun by Dr. John Brockenbrough in 1818. At that time it was just two stories high; the front and rear porches were adorned with Ionic and Doric columns, respectively, and a parapet encompassed the extensive flat roof. During the mid-1850's, however, tho building was "Victorianized." A third story was added, above which a small louvered cupola was installed, and the parapet around the front portion of the house was eliminated.

Of particular note in the interior of the house are the elaborately fashioned brass gilt chandeliers. Representatives of the High Victorian style, they were installed about five years after piped coal gas was made available to Richmond residents in 1851.

Opposed by ambitious politicians and feuding generals during the war, Davis tenaciously refused to allow his government to collapse. Davis and his cabinet remained in Richmond until April 3, 1865, when General Robert E. Lee's abandonment of Petersburg forced Davis to move the Confederate capital to Danville, Virginia. He was captured May 10 in Georgia and imprisoned for two years under degrading conditions. Davis, who was never brought to trial, was released in 1868, his health shattered.

The house in Richmond was occupied for five years after the war by the Federal Government and served as Central School for 20 years. Finally, in 1893, the house was saved from ruin by the Confederate Memorial Literary Society which restored the building and opened it as the Confederate Museum, a treasure house of "things Confederate." Here are Robert E. Lee's sword, the original Great Seal and provisional constitution of the Confederacy, and worn uniforms and faded letters, money and tattered flags — reminders of a noble leader and a lost but honorable cause.

THE HERMITAGE
HERMITAGE, TENNESSEE

"Old Hickory" and His Lady

The Hermitage was the home of Andrew Jackson, seventh President of the United States, hero of the Battle of New Orleans and Tennessee's greatest and most renowned son.

Andrew Jackson was a national figure, generally recognized as one of the nation's greatest Presidents. He was of Scots-Irish descent, born March 15, 1767, in Lancaster County, South Carolina, the son of Andrew and Elizabeth Hutchinson Jackson of Carrickfergus, Ireland.

Jackson's father died before he was born. Brought up during the stormy and desolate years of the American Revolution, he learned to regard the British as implacable enemies during the harsh struggle that took the lives of his mother and two brothers.

The extent of his formal education is not known, but he attended several schools in the Waxhaw area and was probably well educated for his time and place. As a young man, Jackson was a hard worker, aggressive and a fine judge of horseflesh. He studied law and applied himself so earnestly that by the time he was 20 he was licensed to practice law.

Jackson's marriage to Rachel Donelson Robards was one of considerable controversy. They were

The Hermitage: Route 1, Hermitage, Tennessee. Open to the public.

Above: Andrew Jackson's Hermitage has the distinction of being the only national shrine furnished completely with original pieces. Various parts of the estate are planted with trees obtained from the sites of his military campaigns.

married in 1791 and not until two years later, in the fall of 1793, did they learn that Rachel had never been legally divorced from her first husband, Captain Lewis Robards. At first Jackson opposed a second wedding, but in January 1794, they were married a second time. The couple was considered blameless in all the events surrounding their courtship and marriage, but Jackson's political enemies never let him forget.

Jackson's achievements as a military commander won him national recognition and put him on the road to the White House. He emerged from the War of 1812 as the most able field commander in the country and earned the nickname, "Old Hickory," for his firm resolution and daring. His defeat of the British at the Battle of New Orleans restored the military pride of the nation, made the Mississippi an American river and turned the eyes of Americans toward the Pacific.

The Florida campaign of 1818 ended Jackson's military career. In June 1821, Jackson resigned from the army to accept the Governorship of the Florida Territory he had won in the campaign.

In October 1823, the Tennessee legislature elected Jackson United States Senator, and it was while serving in this office that he first became a candidate for the Presidency in 1824. In this election Jackson received the largest number of popular votes, but since no candidate had a majority, the winner was decided by the House of Representatives, which chose John Quincy Adams.

In 1828, by an overwhelming vote, Adams was defeated by Jackson. Before he could be inaugurated, however, Mrs. Jackson died suddenly and was buried in the Hermitage garden.

As President, Jackson allied himself with Daniel Webster in opposition to the nullification doctrine; won the battle opposing the existence of the Bank of the United States; and paid the national debt.

The original Hermitage was built in 1819 and was a brick structure, probably designed by Jackson himself. In this unpretentious home Jackson and his wife lived for nine years until Rachel's death. In 1831, while Jackson was President, the Hermitage was extensively remodeled and improved, but in 1834, the roof of the Hermitage caught fire and much of the building was lost. Although a financial blow to him, Jackson had the home rebuilt.

Jackson died in 1845 and left an estate which was worth $150,000, a considerable amount in those days. Andrew Jackson, Jr., although a kind man, was not a good manager and the property slipped from him. The Hermitage and its 625 acres is now maintained by the Ladies Hermitage Association, organized in 1889 to preserve the estate.

Outstanding about the Hermitage, aside from its stately appearance and manicured, British-designed garden, is that it is the only national shrine furnished completely with original pieces. From the skeletal frame of Jackson's Phaeton carriage, on display in the Carriage House, to a Parisian marble vase in the front parlor, every piece of furniture, china and tapestry — throughout the 12-room house was witness to the passing career of the Tennessee-bred general and President. Two of the most significant display pieces in the house are the im-ported French wallpaper of the entrance hall and a clock in the rear parlor. Surviving over 135 years, the wallpaper depicts the legend of the travels of Telemachus in search of Ulysses; and the clock, one of the oldest relics in the house, is set at the hour Jackson died.

Perhaps the most touching reminder of the Jackson presence at the Hermitage, however, is the inscription on Mrs. Jackson's tomb, composed by her husband, which reads in part: "Her face was fair, her person pleasing, her temper amiable, her heart kind... she thanked the Creator for being permitted to do good. A being so gentle and so virtuous, slander might wound, but could not dishonor...."

OLD GOVERNOR'S MANSION
MILLEDGEVILLE, GEORGIA
Focal Point for Georgia's History

The building of the Old Governor's Mansion was authorized by an act of the Georgia legislature in 1835. It is one of the more perfect and imposing examples of Greek Revival architecture in the South.

Patterned after Palladio's Villa, the home of the Foscari family of Venice, the mansion took three years to complete and cost $50,000. The two architects, John Pell and C. B. Mc Clusky, each were paid a fee of $100 for the plan. The builder was Timothy Porter of Connecticut.

The executive mansion is 60 feet square. Its outside walls of masonry, covered with pink stucco, were recently restored to their original condition. The commanding feature of the interior of the building is a central rotunda lighted by a skylight at the top of a dome plaster-coffered with gold decoration. Projecting into the central rotunda is a circular top-floor balcony with cantilevered supports.

A total of ten governors occupied the mansion between 1839 and 1868. The house was closely associated with Georgia history during the ante-

Above: In addition to the ten governors who resided in the Old Governor's Mansion between 1839 and 1868, General William T. Sherman used this building as his headquarters during his devastating march from Atlanta to the sea in the Civil War.

Old Governor's Mansion: Georgia College, Milledgeville, Georgia. Open to the public.

bellum, Civil War and Reconstruction periods. It was the scene of births, marriages and parties for the many families who resided there. General Sherman used it as his headquarters in November 1864, during his destructive "March to the Sea" through Georgia. It was there that Governor Joseph Emerson Brown was arrested by Federal soldiers in 1865.

The mansion's original furnishings were acquired slowly over many years and when the building ceased to be used as the governor's residence, these furnishings just as slowly were moved from the house and disappeared. The mansion itself fell into a decline. During the 1870's the state rented the building to various local people. At one time it was used as a flop-house where one could stay overnight for as little as 25 cents.

After Georgia Military and Agricultural College was chartered in 1879, the mansion became a dormitory for cadets. Ten years later the state transferred the building and grounds to the Board of Directors of Georgia College at Milledgeville. The building provided the college president and his family with an apartment as well as accommodations for 54 girls. For more than 50 years the mansion served as a dormitory as well as the president's home and reception center.

Immediately upon becoming president in 1956, Dr. Robert E. Lee and his wife began an aggressive drive to restore the mansion furnishings and interiors. In 1965 a complete renovation was started. The State of Georgia provided the funds for the structural work, but the furnishings were completed as a result of gifts from interested citizens, foundations and businesses.

This historic monument, the former home of some of Georgia's greatest men and now part of the Georgia College campus, has played multiple roles. It is an exceptional symbol representing culture, stability and a heritage to which Georgians are deeply attached.

THE
WILLIAM FAULKNER HOME
OXFORD, MISSISSIPPI
Rowan Oak

There is an old Welsh legend of which William Faulkner was particularly fond which claimed that, wherever it grew, the Rowan oak tree would keep away all evil. When he and his wife bought a house situated deep in a woodland of magnificent oak trees they named the place Rowan Oak.

William Faulkner lived and worked at Rowan Oak from 1930 until his death in 1962 and produced the major portion of his work here.

Rowan Oak, intact since 1840, was built by Robert Shegog, a trader, who was among the first pioneers to settle in the Chickasaw country. Originally a primitive farmhouse, the Faulkners made improvements and additions while taking great care to retain the original architectural lines.

The house, facing south, is reached by a driveway lined with ancient cedars and hundreds of iris which grow beneath their branches. A wide brick walk from the front steps meets the driveway.

The wood part of the front gallery is the same as when the house was built, but the brick terraces and bannisters found on either side were added by the Faulkners. Directly south of the driveway and bordering it is an immense circle where three giant magnolia trees cast a deep shade.

William Faulkner loved the view and the warm air of Rowan Oak. He liked to sit on the west gallery terrace, but as he became more widely known he was often disturbed by the strangers who stared at him as he sat there. To help diminish the disturbance, Mrs. Faulkner had a brick wall built enclosing a garden which surrounds the east gallery.

On the north side of the residence, a building, called the Carriage House, was in constant use

William Faulkner Home: 719 Garfield Avenue, Oxford, Mississippi. Not open to the public.

after the Faulkners moved to Rowan Oak. Built by Shegog of home-baked brick, the east room was used by Faulkner for a smoke house where he liked to cure his own hams and bacon and sausage. The west room was used as a toolhouse. To the north of the Carriage House is the house Faulkner built for the servants. The oldest building on the estate is the barn, erected with square-cut notched logs and tightly chinked to make it weatherproof. West of the barn and across the paddock are the stables which William Faulkner built himself.

When the Faulkners bought Rowan Oak, the west front room was immediately designated the library, and it was here that Faulkner did his writing until 1954 when a new addition was built and his office was added.

Across the west hall directly opposite the library is the sanctum sanctorum of Rowan Oak. This was Faulkner's office, a place exclusively his own where horse liniment and tobacco pouch could be placed side by side without ever being disturbed. In this office, along with the many of his personal effects, Faulkner left what many distinguished scholars call the most famous literary wall in the world. On it is the complex outline of his book, *A Fable*, which is an allegorical novel about mutiny in the front lines during World War I.

The house and grounds as a whole seem to evoke something of the sense of the man who so recently lived there, the man who said in his Nobel Prize acceptance speech that "man will prevail."

Below: Nobel Prize-winner William Faulkner did much writing at his shaded Rowan Oak estate, named for the legendary tree which is supposed to dispel all evil. A wall of his study is papered with the outline for his book, A Fable.

IV MIDWESTERN HOUSES

JEAN BAPTISTE SAUCIER HOUSE
CAHOKIA, ILLINOIS
France in the Upper Mississippi Valley

The Cahokia Court House, located southeast of St. Louis in St. Clair County, Illinois, was at one time the home of Jean Baptiste Saucier, the French engineer who built neighboring Fort Des Chartres in 1753. Constructed sometime after 1737, this four-room structure is an accurate example of the French pioneer log building, and is considered to be the oldest private dwelling and courthouse anywhere in the Midwest.

The Jean Baptiste Saucier House is preserved on its original site in a park area which covers about four city blocks. Representative of the period in which it was constructed, the log structure has a cantilever roof which extends down over the porches and the interstices are filled with stone and mortar. Resting on a stone foundation two feet thick, the building is nearly square, measuring 35 feet by 43 feet-eight inches.

When this building was erected, Cahokia — which dates to 1699, and is the oldest permanent settlement in the Mississippi Valley — was part of the French Province of Louisiana. Founded by three missionaries from the foreign missions of Quebec,

Canada, the settlement saw only 12 white men amid the surrounding Cahokia Indian population by 1723. However, sometime before this land was ceded to the British in 1763, following the French and Indian War, Cahokia became the largest of the French Mississippi River towns with over 3,000 residents.

In 1790 St. Clair County was organized as part of the Northwest Territory and the county seat was established at Cahokia. Three years later the Jean Baptiste Saucier house was purchased and became the first court house in the Midwest. Using the four rooms of the building as a courtroom, jail and administrative offices, the jurisdictional limits of this newly formed government seat extended from what is now southern Illinois to the Canadian border.

By 1814, however, the constant threat of floods from the Mississippi River induced government officials to move their capital to Belleville. For a period of nearly 100 years after this, the old court house was used as a saloon, storehouse, meeting hall and a private residence.

With the 1904 Louisiana Purchase Exposition, the house was dismantled and moved to the St.

Jean Baptiste Saucier House: Cahokia, Illinois. Open to the public.

Above: The John Baptiste Saucier House is considered to be the oldest private residence in the Midwest. Below: A 1925 mural depicts Gen. Arthur St. Clair addressing Cahokia residents sometime after the Revolution.

Louis fair grounds as a display. At the conclusion of the exposition, the building was sold to the Chicago Historical Society, and one-fourth of the original court house was set up on the Wooded Island of Jackson Park in Chicago.

In 1938, under the Works Progress Administration, the Cahokia Memorial Survey was started which brought the courthouse back to its colonial site. In excavations carried out that summer, the original foundation was uncovered, as well as fragments of iron work and domestic objects. Reconstructing the building from old photographs and sketches, using as much of the original materials as remained, the home of the Mississippi Valley's first court trials and elections was preserved at the original site after 124 years of neglect and nomadic wanderings.

LOUIS BOLDUC HOUSE
STE. GENEVIEVE, MISSOURI
French Colonial Missouri

The Louis Bolduc house at Ste. Genevieve, Missouri, has been preserved as the first authentic example of an essentially complete French colonial home in the Mississippi Valley. Its builder, a French-Canadian immigrant who could neither read nor write, settled in the old village of Ste. Genevieve, Missouri, in 1740, where he became one of the wealthiest men in the territory through mining and commercial enterprises.

When the Mississippi River overflowed its banks in 1785, Louis Bolduc moved his house, along with the rest of the village, to the present site of Ste. Genevieve. The Bolduc family had occupied the house for five generations when it was acquired by the National Society of the Colonial Dames of America and opened as a museum in 1957.

Restored to its original appearance, the Bolduc House is a product of two distinct architectural origins. The basic structure, a rectangular unit consisting of two large rooms separated by a central hall, was styled after the Norman farmhouses of the French countryside. The addition of a hipped, cantilever roof, extending on all sides of the house to form an exterior gallery, demonstrates the French acquaintance with West Indian styles.

The frame of the house was constructed from hand-hewn oak timbers, set upright on a stone foundation, a type of construction referred to as posts-on-a-sill (*poteaux-sur-solle*) in French colonial deed records. Between the timbers, interstices were packed with a nogging of clay and chopped straw and, above, heavy oak tresses of French medieval descent supported the roof. In the restoration, the exterior of the house was covered with whitewash derived from an old formula found in the Ste. Genevieve archives.

Despite the adherence to authentic detail and the availability of many of the original materials, the extent of the grounds has been reduced substantially and accompanying facilities are complete reconstructions.

The house is surrounded by a palisade of six-foot cedar posts in the manner of those from which early settlers repelled intruding Indians and later protected their property against the flow of cattle along narrow streets. Within this enclosure there is a stone building, originally used as a bake house before a kitchen was added to the northwest corner of the gallery in 1820. Subsequently this structure served as a smokehouse for meats. A grape arbor, orchard and garden, containing many of the herbs used by the colonial community, have also been reproduced.

Ste. Genevieve is believed to have been a mid-18th-century extension of the Cahokia, Illinois, settlement where other historic houses have been restored. In these restorations, accomplished prior to the work of the Colonial Dames at Ste. Genevieve, the Bolduc House was often used for reference when building records, or structures themselves, were incomplete or had been altered.

Louis Bolduc House: Sainte Genevieve, Missouri. Open to the public. Color illustration, p. 146.

Above: The Louis Bolduc House is one of the earliest examples of French colonial architecture in the Mississippi Valley. Built initially around 1740, it was moved to its present Ste. Genevieve site when the Mississippi overflowed in 1785.

RUFUS PUTNAM HOUSE
MARIETTA, OHIO
New England in the Midwest

Three years after the signing of the Treaty of Paris in 1783, which formally ended the Revolutionary War, there was born, at a Boston tavern called the Bunch of Grapes, a plan which resulted in the introduction of New England architecture in the Midwest. At this tavern General Rufus Putnam organized a group of Revolutionary War veterans into the Ohio Company of Associates, and later secured a million and a half acres of land in the Northwest Territory.

In 1787 the Continental Congress established civil control over this tract; and the next year Putnam and 47 followers established the first authorized United States settlement in the territory. Located at the mouth of the Muskingum River, the pioneer community was named Marietta, honoring the French Queen Marie Antoinette for her country's aid in the War of Independence.

Above: The Rufus Putnam House, now enclosed in the Campus Martius Museum, is the only remaining structure of the Campus Martius settlement started by General Rufus Putnam and his Ohio Company of Associates after the Revolution.

Rufus Putnam House: Campus Martius Museum, Marietta, Ohio. Open to the public.

141

When Putnam arrived at Marietta, Indian upheavals in the Ohio Territory dictated much of the architectural style. Fort Harmer, established at the direction of General Josiah Harmer who was to suffer a humiliating defeat at the hands of the Indians in 1790, was across the Muskingum River from the new settlement and afforded little protection. For this reason, Marietta was begun as a fortified village on a bluff above the river which its builders called "Campus Martius," a Latin phrase which means "Field of Mars."

The fortification consisted of four blockhouses situated at each corner of a 144-foot perimeter. These buildings were 18 feet square and were designed to accommodate newly arrived settlers, to serve for public functions and to provide defense. The space remaining between the blockhouses was partitioned into building lots which were leased to individual members of the community for a period of 20 years. Lessees were then required to build adjoining homes, the exterior walls of which would connect the blockhouses and form a stockade.

General Putnam's house was among the first completed residences in the fortified village. Its design, along with the other buildings, was typically New England, modified to meet frontier conditions and necessities. A two-story, four-room, gabled structure of hand-hewn timbers joined by mortise and tenon, the simple frame house reflected the architectural style and structural detail which the early colonists had inherited from medieval England. With the urgency to complete the fortification, green planks placed horizontally were used as walls. The planks later shrank which necessitated packing the cracks with lath until clapboards could be added. At great expense and sacrifice, General Putnam transported furniture, HL hinges, putty and window glass over long distances in an effort to maintain the essence of New England construction and domestic life. The result is a style known as "Frontier Colonial Vernacular."

In 1795, Campus Martius was razed. General "Mad Anthony" Wayne had subdued the Indians the year before at the Battle of Fallen Timbers, and the signing of the Treaty of Greeneville made the fort unnecessary. Putnam was apparently the only member of the original Ohio Company to retain his house, to which he added four more rooms sometime after 1796.

More than a century later, in 1917, the house was acquired by the Ohio General Assembly as a historic memorial of the Ohio Historical Society. Today, as the oldest structure still existing in the area of the Old Northwest, the dwelling is enclosed in one wing of the Campus Martius Museum. The Ohio Land Company Office, contemporaneous to the Putnam House, is also on the museum grounds.

GROUSELAND

VINCENNES, INDIANA

White House of the West

When William Henry Harrison built the house he called Grouseland in 1804, he was Governor of the Indiana Territory, a land mass larger than that occupied by all the states at that time. Initially this territory included only the present states of Indiana, Illinois, Michigan, Wisconsin and eastern Minnesota; but with the Louisiana Purchase of 1803, its boundaries were expanded to include Missouri, Arkansas, Iowa, western Minnesota, Kansas, Nebraska, Colorado, North Dakota, South Dakota, Montana, Wyoming and Oklahoma. Although this expansive domain was short-lived as the Indiana Territory, Grouseland, from which Harrison ministered his official duties, became known as the "White House of the West."

Located along the upper reaches of the Wabash River at Vincennes, Indiana, Grouseland was constructed in a walnut grove after the Georgian style of tidewater Virginia. It is a spacious, two-story brick structure with false windows, secret passages

Grouseland: 3 West Scott Street, Vincennes, Indiana. Open to the public.

MIDWESTERN HOUSES

*Above: In 1865 Ulysses S. Grant was presented this
handsome two-story brick residence in Galena, Illinois,
by private citizens as a tribute to the victorious general.
For many years the bearded Grant and his Japanese servant were familiar figures on Galena's streets.*

Above: President Lincoln's desk is one of the original furnishings in the Springfield home which provides a nucleus for the authentic restoration. Several pieces of the family's household goods were unfortunately lost in Chicago's great fire of 1871.

144

Phil McCafferty

*Above: A simple two-room cottage in the village of
West Branch, Iowa, was the birthplace of Herbert Hoover
in 1874. His humble origin on the banks of the Wapsinonoc
left an indelible impression upon this man whose
long life was devoted to humanitarian goals.*

*Left: Abraham Lincoln's Springfield home is depicted
in a print which appeared between 1861 and 1865. Here
he brought his wife and infant son, Robert Todd, in 1844.
Three of his other sons were born in the home
and one, Eddie, died there in 1850.*

145

Left: The 57-room Octagon House in Watertown, Wisconsin, reflects a unique style of architecture which flourished in America before the Civil War. Its many advanced features probably inspired the "House of Tomorrow" at Chicago's 1933 Century of Progress Exhibition.

Below: The 197-year-old Louis Bolduc House in Ste. Genevieve, Missouri, remains as one of the largest and most characteristic French colonial houses extant. Sparse furnishings in the living room reflect the early days of Missouri history when even necessities were luxuries.

(Continued from page 142)

and the legend of a tunnel somewhere on the grounds, even though there is no evidence to support this assertion.

It was built during a time of upheaval among the Indians, and is noted for having been the site where five treaties were signed with northern tribes. Among the many distinguished visitors to Grouseland were the Indian Chief Tecumseh and his brother the Prophet, who came to utter their dissatisfaction over the cession of Indian lands.

Standing in the midst of the walnut grove before the mansion, Tecumseh is reputed to have charged: "Sell a country! Why not sell the air, the clouds and the great sea, as well as the earth? Did not the great spirit make them all for the use of his children?"

Discouraged with the endless treaties, Tecumseh did not return to Grouseland after 1811. In the fall of that year Harrison met and defeated Tecumseh at Tippecanoe Creek. Harrison's campaign slogan, "Tippecanoe and Tyler too," in his Presidential election victory of 1840 was a reference to that battle. A more important battlefield triumph for Harrison, however, took place in October 1813, near the Thames River in Canada, north of Lake Erie. This time Tecumseh was slain and troops lead by Harrison captured an entire British force. As a result, the United States was in undisputed possession of the Great Lakes except for Lake Ontario.

In 1812 Harrison had moved his family back to his country home in North Bend, Ohio, and he resigned as governor. After the conclusion of the war in 1814, he resigned his command and returned to Ohio. Harrison remained there until he achieved the Presidency in 1840, when he defeated Martin Van Buren.

For a period of about four or five years after the war, the house at Grouseland was occupied by Judge Benjamin Parke, reverting back to the Harrison family in 1819 when Harrison's son, John Cleves Symmes Harrison, settled there with his family. In 1850 the house passed out of the family for the last time, and was used as a hotel and a granary until 1860, when it again became a residence.

In 1909 the Vincennes Water Company bought the house and was about to destroy it when the Francis Vigo Chapter of the Daughters of the American Revolution intervened. Raising funds to preserve the house, the D. A. R. opened it to the public in 1910, and in 1949 some restoration work was done. It wasn't until 1963, however, that extensive restoration was begun. Every effort was made at that time to restore Grouseland to look as it did during the time William Henry and his wife Anna lived there. For this reason, none of the furnishings in the house today are of later origin than 1812.

Below: When William Henry Harrison built the house he called Grouseland, it became known as the "White House of the West." At that time he was the appointed Governor of the Indiana Territory, an area larger than all of the states combined.

W.M. Cline Company

ADENA

(Thomas Worthington House,)

CHILLICOTHE, OHIO

Latrobe Along the Ohio

Thomas Worthington built his Midwestern country home between 1806 and 1807, having been drawn out of his native Virginia by the beauty of the Ohio country nine years earlier. With his wife, Eleanor, he settled near Chillicothe, then the capital of the Northwest Territory, and prospered in land speculation, grist, saw and cotton mills, iron and coal prospecting, stock farming and river shipping.

Through these successful enterprises, he achieved great political influence and, in the years preceding 1803, played an important role in gaining statehood for Ohio. His brother-in-law, Edward Tiffin, was the state's first governor and Worthington was one of its first United States Senators. In the years following, he served both as governor and state legislator.

Constructed on more than 1,500 acres of land overlooking Chillicothe, Worthington's estate was designed by a prominent architect-engineer Benjamin Latrobe, considered to be the father of the Federal style. The main house consists of a large, colonnaded central structure, joined on either side by two smaller wings. Formal gardens east of the mansion contain an abundance of roses known to have grown in America early in the 19th century.

Outbuildings for the mansion included an ice house, smoke house, wash house and servants' quarters. Stable facilities were added in a ravine to the northwest. The completed estate stood at the opening of the Scioto Valley which stretches out to meet Mount Logan, the view depicted in Ohio's State Seal.

In the first years of his residence there, Worthington chose to call the estate Mt. Prospect Hall, but in 1812 he changed the name to "Adena," a Hebrew word denoting paradise.

Some of the original furnishings remain in the house today, but most of the pieces, although authentic representatives of the period, are careful substitutions. Sheraton and Hepplewhite designs dominate the colonial motif with a few articles of Chippendale and Duncan Phyfe and one or two innovations designed by Worthington himself. The woodwork has been repainted with original colors, similar to those in Colonial Williamsburg. Contemporary wallpaper designs have also been reproduced.

In the state dining room, along with the numerous pieces of silverware produced by local artisans, there is a revolving circular cabinet generally attributed to Worthington. Built into the wall between the state dining room and the family dining room, this cupboard of five shelves revolves on a center pin and was used to transport the meal service between the two rooms. Worthington installed another circular cupboard in the drawing room to serve afternoon tea and other light refreshments. A more subtle, but nonetheless creative, article of the Worthington family is a red and green silk sampler which hangs in the first-floor bedroom. Eleanor Worthington is reputed to have made this in 1790, when she was 13 years old. A unique commode chest also was Mrs. Worthington's.

One remaining article of unusual interest from this historic mansion is a ceremonial tomahawk. Displayed on the mantelpiece of the study, the tomahawk was presented to Worthington as a token of friendship by the Shawnee chief, Tecumseh, six years prior to his death at the Battle of the Thames. The coffin in which Worthington was buried is probably the only casket in the country known as a Duncan Phyfe original. The noted furniture-maker was commissioned to do the coffin in 1827 at a cost of $70, as evidenced by the original bill, one of the few known bills signed by Phyfe.

Adena: Allen Avenue, Chillicothe, Ohio. Open to the public. Color illustration, p. 163.

Above: The Old Fauntleroy House, known simply as "No. 53" by the early Rappite settlers, is one of the few remnants of a communal culture begun on the Wabash River around 1814. It later became the site of the first American women's club.

THE OLD FAUNTLEROY HOUSE
NEW HARMONEY,
INDIANA
Visionaries in Indiana

The historic village of New Harmoney, Indiana, founded by Father George Rapp, an immigrant minister from Germany, was originally an extension of European attempts to overcome the evils of the industrial revolution through the visionary bliss of communal living. Established around 1814 on the Wabash River, New Harmoney was the second such village founded by the Harmonists and is the site of the Old Fauntleroy House, designated simply as "No. 53" when it was built by the Harmonist settlers.

By 1824, life had become very easy and Father Rapp decided to move his colony once again. That year, he sold the 30,000-acre New Harmoney settle-ment to Robert Dale Owen, a Scottish industrialist and social reformer. Owen continued the communal tradition at New Harmoney for awhile; but by 1828, the failure of the reform experiment was imminent. In spite of this, the settlement continued to grow, the solid structures left by the Harmonists serving as the foundation for an active and vigorous community.

Constructed from hand-hewn timbers of hickory, oak and walnut, No. 53 was typical of the Harmonist buildings. The beams, some of which are 30 feet long and 12 inches square, are joined securely by mortise and tenon and maul-driven pegs. The roof is gabled north and south, and floors and weather

The Old Fauntleroy House: New Harmoney State Memorial, Indiana. Open to the public.

boarding are laid in poplar. Each of the five original rooms was outfitted with handcrafted brass door knobs, locks and keys.

Eleven years after the denouement of the second New Harmoney experiment, No. 53 was sold at a public auction to Robert H. Fauntleroy, who had previously married Jane Owen, only daughter of Robert Dale Owen. As an indirect result of this marriage, a portion of the social reform sought by New Harmoney settlers was realized, and No. 53 was redesignated as the Fauntleroy House.

Although Robert and Jane Fauntleroy attempted no social reform on their own, a daughter, Constance, unknowingly provided the impetus for one of the biggest social revolutions in our history. Less zealous than her grandfather, Constance merely organized a

women's group called the Minerva Club. This is reputed to have been the first women's club in America, and it was created solely as a literary society. Nonetheless, from these humble beginnings in 1859, the idea of organized societies spread throughout the country as a means to emancipate women and win them equal rights. In 1925 the last descendant of the Fauntleroy family to hold the house sold it to the Indiana Federation of Women's Clubs as a shrine for women's organizations.

The women's federation retained the house until 1955, when title was transferred to the State of Indiana; and No. 53 was incorporated into a state memorial to the historic traditions of the New Harmoney settlers.

Below: The Taft House has been a prominent part of the American artistic community since it was built in 1820. Murals in the main entrance hall, painted by Scots-Negro artist Robert Duncanson, had been lost beneath layers of wallpaper.

THE TAFT HOUSE

CINCINNATI, OHIO

The Tafts of Ohio

From 1820, when Martin Baum built the residence at first known as Belmont and later as the Taft House, it seemed destined to secure a prominent position in American artistic, cultural and political tradition.

The identity of the architect is unknown, but the building is one of the best remaining examples of Federal architecture, styled after homes built in Virginia and Maryland during the early years of the Republic. Designed with a high central unit which is flanked by two lower wings, the Taft House — which was converted to a museum in 1932 — is representative of the Federal taste for spacious, formal parlors and a ballroom, forming a contrast with the more compact bedroom facilities in the wings. What was once the ground floor carriage entrance, adjoined by the kitchen, service area and the servants' dining room, is now the main visitor entrance and display hall for temporary exhibitions. Adding to the authentic atmosphere of the museum are the furnishings which have been preserved from the actual period of the building. Antique printed cottons and satins adorn many of the walls, and the collection of Duncan Phyfe furniture is representative of his early work.

Martin Baum was afforded little more than the opportunity of building the house before he was overcome by the financial upheavals of 1819-1820; but succeeding owners transformed the Cincinnati residence into a center of flourishing social life and artistic endeavor. Nicholas Longworth, who owned the house from 1830 until 1866, was a loyal patron of the arts, especially the work of the sculptor, Hiram Powers, and a Scots-Negro artist, Robert Duncanson. Duncanson's only known murals were uncovered in the entrance hall during the restoration of 1931, surviving nearly a century after being covered with wallpaper and several coats of varnish.

In 1871 the house was sold to David Sinton, reputed to be the wealthiest man in Cincinnati at the time. He and his daughter Anna occupied the house, continuing its growing tradition, until sometime after 1873, the year that Anna married Charles Phelps Taft, half-brother of the future President William Howard Taft.

Charles Phelps Taft was the first son of Alphonso Taft, a noted lawyer who settled in Cincinnati in 1840. Originally from Vermont, the elder Taft established the foundation for the dynasty of lawyers, statesmen and public servants that was to follow and which is still active today. During the last years of the Grant administration, Alphonso reached the heights of his career, serving both as Secretary of War and Attorney General. With a $50,000 stipend from his grandfather, Charles followed his father's law career and, after his marriage to Anna Sinton, became the keystone of the aspiring Taft family.

Publisher, congressman and philanthropist, Charles Taft enthusiastically accumulated a collection of art and unique artifacts which characterized the best craftsmanship of America, Europe and the Far East. Among the many masters to be viewed throughout the historic mansion are Rembrandt, Turner, Goya, Gainsborough and Corot. In addition, there are rare tapestries and textiles, Renaissance Limoges enamels, jewelry and other artifacts, representing a variety of nations and periods, as well as a 200-piece collection of Chinese porcelain.

In an effort to preserve this collection and the authentic atmosphere of the house, Mr. and Mrs. Taft donated their art, home and a grant of $1,000,000 to the citizens of Cincinnati in 1927. With the contribution, however, there was a stipulation requiring the citizens to fund another $2,500,000, which led subsequently to the formation of the Cincinnati Institute of Fine Arts. As the nucleus of the institute, the museum was formally dedicated in 1932, preserving a cultural tradition begun over 100 years earlier in the names of Charles Phelps and Anna Sinton Taft.

The Taft Museum: 316 Pike Street, Cincinnati, Ohio. Open to the public. Color illustrations, pp. 164, 165.

INDIAN AGENCY HOUSE
PORTAGE, WISCONSIN
Life on the Wisconsin Frontier

The site of old Fort Winnebago and the Indian Agency House is a mile-wide stretch of land originally used as a portage by boatmen, changing their cargo from the Fox to the Wisconsin River. Father Marquette and Louis Jolliet are reputed to have used this portage as early as 1673 when they traveled through the Northwest Territory.

Years later, when the Winnebago Indians ceded these lands to the United States Government, an agency was established here for the purpose of enforcing the treaty and supervising the Indians, distributing their annual stipend and serving as a guardian to wards of the Government. In 1832, John H. Kinzie, appointed as Indian Agent three years earlier, was allowed, by the Government, to build the Agency House at a cost of $3,997.18. He spent only a short time there, leaving on July 1, 1833. A book entitled *Wau-Bun,* written years later by his wife Juliette, portrays the house as a center

of pioneer social life, and describes the Kinzies' relationship to the Winnebago Indians.

Much of this social activity was apparently conducted around a piano which Mrs. Kinzie transported from New York. In *Wau-Bun* she wrote of weekly musicales conducted with soldiers, Indians and Canadian interpreters. The original piano is no longer in existence, but one made by the same firm about 1832 has been placed on display in the house.

Life at The Portage, however, was not entirely joyous. Mrs. Kinzie also recalled the first months at the agency when the Indians, anticipating removal from their lands, had failed to cultivate their crops: "We were soon obliged to keep both doors and windows fast, to shut out the sight of misery we could not relieve. . . .They would climb up on the outside and tier upon tier of gaunt, wretched faces would peer in above to watch us, and see if indeed we were as ill-provided . . . ."

Indian Agency House: Portage, Wisconsin. Open to the public.

Below: The piano in the parlor of the Indian Agency House is an 1832 replica of the one which Mrs. John H. Kinzie transported from New York after her husband was appointed to administer the Winnebago Indian Reservation in the 19th century.

With the exception of the surgeon's quarters of Fort Winnebago, the Agency House is the only surviving member of that early complex of buildings. The fort buildings, constructed by the soldiers, were made of boards cut from green logs which were inclined to warp and crack after being set in place. The soldiers plugged the resulting crevices with cotton batting and pasted strips of paper. The Agency House, on the other hand, had both an inner and outer wall, in between which was constructed another wall of solid brick.

In 1932, 100 years after the house was built, it was restored by The National Society of the Colonial Dames of America in the State of Wisconsin as a museum house with furnishings of the period. These are the kinds of things the Kinzies would have had, but are not the original ones owned by them, because when they left the Indian Agency House, they went to Chicago, where their furniture was destroyed by the fire of 1871.

Despite the respect he gained from the Indians, Kinzie left The Portage on July 1, 1833. He had expected the agency to control the largest Indian population in the Northwest Territory, excepting only Chicago, and that it would be raised from a sub-agency to one of independent status. When this did not happen and the Government refused to grant him a raise in salary, Kinzie resigned.

THE
SIBLEY HOUSE
MENDOTA, MINNESOTA
Gathering Place in the Minnesota Territory

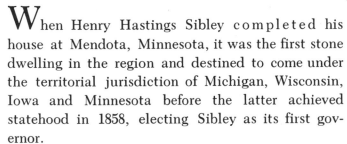

When Henry Hastings Sibley completed his house at Mendota, Minnesota, it was the first stone dwelling in the region and destined to come under the territorial jurisdiction of Michigan, Wisconsin, Iowa and Minnesota before the latter achieved statehood in 1858, electing Sibley as its first governor.

Sometimes called the Mount Vernon of Minnesota, this limestone structure reaches a height of 17 feet at the ceiling of the second story, sheltering a small attic beneath its gabled roof and a cellar of vaulted storage rooms beneath the ground floor. Wooden pegs join the hand-hewn timbers in the frame from which several partitions were constructed by fitting smaller, horizontal beams between the upright timbers and packing the resulting spaces with an interlacing of willow branches and clay. The ceilings were constructed in much the same manner, and the roof was shingled with hand-split, oak clapboards. That this old house survived subsequent owners and abuse, however, was due mainly to the solidarity of the stone of both the inner and outer walls. Stones for the house were quarried locally in blocks two-and-

a-half-feet thick.

Drawn to the Minnesota Territory as a representative of the American Fur Company, Sibley was able to boast other firsts in his Mendota home. As a businessman, he brought with him a vault of a variety unknown before in that part of the country and, after his marriage in 1843, his wife imported the first piano. Many of these possessions remained after Sibley's departure in 1862. However, some substitution was required to obtain furnishings from that period, when the Minnesota D.A.R. undertook restoration of that mansion in 1910.

Besides the architectural significance of the Sibley house and its importance as the home of an early American political leader, it is also noteworthy for its role as a gathering place for a great number and variety of travelers and traders. Sibley once remarked, "I have often had from 20 to 30 at my table at a time, who, of course were not charged anything. All who came were welcome, provided they were good fellows, and gentlemanly in their tastes and habits."

Among many uninvited, yet welcome, guests were the Sioux Indians who brought furs to trade.

The Sibley House: Sibley Memorial Highway, Mendota, Minnesota. Open to the public.

Climbing an outside staircase to the attic, they were able to use this space as a living quarter until their business was completed. In 1849, Alexander Ramsay, the first Governor of the Minnesota Territory, remained with his family at the Mendota mansion for a month while he awaited suitable quarters at St. Paul. It was at this time that Sibley's study on the first floor became known as the Capitol Room.

There was one guest, however, who managed to exceed the limits of Sibley's liberal hospitality. Captain Frederick Marryat, a British Naval officer and an author well known for his stories of the sea, visited the mansion during the 1830's when the United States and Britain were disputing the boundary of Maine. Refuting the U.S. position and attempting to incite the Sioux Indians to rally to the side of the British if hostilities broke out, Marryat's visit was rapidly concluded when the future governor dismissed him from his house.

Governor Sibley sold his home in 1862 and Sibley House was reduced to ruin by the turn of the century. Its restoration in 1910 brought back again the original charm of the home which was a center of pioneer life in the territorial era.

Above: The Lincoln House in Springfield, Illinois, was designed after the Greek Revival style as it was interpreted on the frontier. The horsehair sofa in the far corner of the parlor is among the original furnishings.

Below: The walls of the Sibley House were constructed from blocks of stone two-and-one-half-feet thick. When Henry Hastings Sibley occupied the house, Indians from neighboring tribes boarded in the third-story attic while they traded their furs.

ABRAHAM LINCOLN HOME

SPRINGFIELD, ILLINOIS

Lincoln's Springfield Years

By 1844, Abraham Lincoln was rapidly approaching political prominence. He had already served four terms in the Illinois State Legislature, participated in two law firms as a junior partner and played an active role in the Presidential campaign of 1840, which brought the Whigs their first victory in the person of William Henry Harrison.

It was in this year that Lincoln bought a one-and-a-half-story cottage for $1,500 from the Reverend Charles Dresser, who had married him to Mary Todd two years earlier. Except for one year (1847) during his term in the United States Congress, Lincoln occupied this house until he left Springfield as President-elect in 1861.

Three of Lincoln's sons were born in this house and one died there. The death of Edward Baker Lincoln in 1850 at the age of four foreshadowed future tragedies that would weigh on the Lincoln family during the Presidential years.

Built in 1839, the two-story frame house, which has been preserved on the original Eighth and Jackson Streets' site, achieved its final form when Mary Todd Lincoln added the extra half-story in 1856. Reflected in its delicate trim and cornices, the house was designed in the Greek Revival style as it appeared on the frontier, framed in oak and sided and floored with black walnut.

Architecturally, it is a modest representative of the pre-Civil War era. What is most meaningful about it is that the purchase of this home marked the division between Lincoln's interest in local and state politics and his embarkation into national affairs. At this time he was on the verge of gaining a seat in the U.S. Congress after two previous and unsuccessful attempts.

Outside of politics, Lincoln was steadily achieving acclaim as one of Illinois' leading lawyers, maintaining that "as a peacemaker the lawyer has a superior opportunity of being a good man." He had been admitted to the bar in 1837 under the

tutelage of John T. Stuart, a successful Springfield lawyer, and went into partnership with him for a period of about four years. This was followed by a shorter term with Stephen T. Logan and, in 1844, Lincoln established his own practice with William H. Herndon as a junior partner.

He obtained a reputation as capable jury lawyer during these years, but his greatest strength lay in the higher courts which depended less on extemporaneous rhetoric. A classic case — disputing the collection of payment for a slave — which he tried only a few years after his admission to the bar appears to support this assertion. A man named Nathan Cromwell had a Negro girl in his service for some years whom he claimed was bound to him by indenture and could be sold as any property. Ultimately, a man named Bailey bought the girl, but agreed to pay only upon receipt of papers stipulating that the girl was bound to service according to the laws of the state. Papers were not served prior to Cromwell's death, however, and later heirs sued for the purchase price. Representing the subsequent Bailey claim against payment, Lincoln lost the case in the lower court; but in a careful presentation before the State Supreme Court, Lincoln proved that there could be no ownership of slaves in a free state, and the suit was dismissed.

In 1846 Lincoln was elected to the U.S. Congress. This was a disheartening period for both Lincoln and his constituents, however, and at the end of the term, Lincoln himself confessed that he would not be able to muster enough support to seek the office a second time. His only notable accomplishment during these two years was an unpopular stand against President Polk's promotion of the Mexican War. Persistently, he demanded that the President prove the war was not a product of United States' aggression.

Even before this debacle in Congress, after which he returned indefinitely to his law practice, there

---

Lincoln Home State Memorial: 420 S. Eighth St., Springfield, Ill. Open to the public. Color illustrations, pp. 144, 145.

were forces at work throughout the country which would preclude his retirement from politics for very long. There was great sectional turmoil over the extension of slavery into the Western territories, and as early as 1837, Lincoln had expressed a strong moral objection to that institution. Therefore, when Stephen A. Douglas, brought a bill before the Senate in 1854, which proposed the admission of Kansas and Nebraska to the Union, granting self-determination on the slavery terms issue, Lincoln reappeared in the Congressional election, campaigning vigorously against the act. By the end of the campaign, Lincoln had gained recognition as the leader of the Illinois "anti-Nebraskans" who would figure heavily in the organization of the Republican Party in 1856.

The first Presidential candidate of the Republicans, John C. Frémont, was defeated by Democrat James Buchanan in that same year. Whatever support there was for the abolitionist movement was counter-balanced by a greater fear over the dissolution of the Union if some compromise were not reached.

In 1858 Senator Douglas was up for re-election. Through his opposition to the Kansas-Nebraska Act and vigorous support of Frémont, Lincoln won the opportunity to oppose Douglas. In the months prior to the election, Lincoln challenged Douglas to a series of public debates which inevitably focused on the slavery issue. In continuous attacks against the Southern slaveholders and Northern liberals, Lincoln told the nation, "Familiarize yourselves with the chains of bondage and you are preparing yourselves to wear them. . . You have lost the genius of your own independence and become fit subjects for the first cunning tyrant who rises among you."

Lincoln lost the election, but he gained politically. With the approach of the 1860 Presidential elections, Lincoln was so closely identified with the slavery issue that he was the natural champion of the Republican cause. Numerical superiority of the free states over the slave states, by this time, assured Lincoln of a majority in a wide field of candidates; and in 1861, as President-elect, he left Illinois forever. Speaking almost prophetically to a group of friends who accompanied him to the railroad station, he said: "Here I have lived for a quarter of a century. . . .Here my children have been born and one is buried. . . .I now leave, not knowing when, or whether ever, I may return. . . ."

Today Lincoln's Springfield house, maintained as a memorial by the State of Illinois, contains some of the original furnishings: Lincoln's hatrack in the downstairs hallway; the dining room has the Lincolns' dessert service on the card table; the reproduced Brussels carpet and horsehair sofa are in the living room; Lincoln's favorite horsehair-covered rocker is in the sitting room; his secretary is in the back parlor; and his shaving mirror and chest of drawers are in his bedroom.

Wisconsin Conservation Dept.

Above: Stained-glass windows were common in the "House on the Mound" of Hercules L. Dousman, Wisconsin's first millionaire. Later renamed Villa Louis, the Dousman monogram is incorporated into the pattern of the glass.

VILLA LOUIS
PRAIRIE DU CHIEN, WISCONSIN

House on the Mound

The present site of Prairie du Chien, Wisconsin's second oldest city, was settled by the Hopewell Indians over 2,000 years ago. In this settlement, the Indians maintained a huge burial mound which was bounded by the Wisconsin and Mississippi Rivers and overlooked the point where they joined. In later years, the military significance of this mound was to have a vital role in the settlement of the northern Mississippi River Valley.

Subsequent to the Marquette-Jolliet expedition through this region in 1673, French, British and American traders and explorers forged the way for colonization. As control of the upper valley passed ultimately to the Americans, each succeeding army occupied fortifications on the strategic piece of ground. The last military stronghold to be established on the site was the first American Fort Crawford, built in 1816. When the fort was abandoned for higher ground in 1829, the ancient burial mound was acquired by Hercules L. Dousman as part of a 4,500-acre estate where Villa Louis would be constructed 14 years later.

Hercules Dousman was both an agent for Jacob Astor's American Fur Company and a successful land speculator. In this last enterprise, it was to his advantage when Andrew Jackson achieved the Presidency in 1828. For Jackson, through his fundamental adherence to a states' rights philosophy, provided the impetus for the wildcat banks which mushroomed throughout the West during the first half of the 19th century. The irresponsible financial practices of these banks enabled many shrewd businessmen to amass large personal fortunes through speculation. As for Dousman, he became Wisconsin's first millionaire.

In 1843 he built his "House on the Mound" along Georgian lines, where he spent the remaining years of his life. Early in the 1870's his widow remodeled much of the house in the mid-Victorian style, but it was the second Mrs. Dousman who renamed the mansion Villa Louis and provided the social atmosphere for which the home gained widespread renown. Throughout these two generations, the house was filled with fine furniture and art objects — hand-carved rosewood chairs, waterford crystal chandeliers, fine china, velvet and satin upholstery and valuable paintings. In addition to the accumulation of the fine furnishings and display articles, the second Mrs. Dousman also administered a great many charitable organizations, creating an almost legendary aura around herself as the patroness of the sick and the needy.

Reportedly, the second Mrs. Dousman had achieved considerable social prominence even before coming to Villa Louis. When she was 20 years old, prior to her marriage, the Grand Duke Alexis of Russia is supposed to have selected her as one of three most beautiful women in America. She then accompanied him on a tour of the Mississippi River.

In this extravagant setting on the Mississippi River, Villa Louis became a center of business and cultural activity in the early Midwest, where politicians, financiers, artists and soldiers were gaily entertained at lavish parties. Accompanying the main house, Dousman built an ice house which provided air conditioning, a wine cellar, a preserve house and a carriage house.

In the 1930's, Mrs. Virginia Dousman Bigelow restored the mansion to its appearance during the time the second and third generations of the Dousman family resided in the home, designating the Carriage House as a museum for Prairie du Chien history and partially reconstructing old Fort Crawford which had originally occupied the site.

Villa Louis: Villa Louis Road, Prairie du Chien, Wisconsin. Open to the public. Color illustration, p. 166.

Above: J. F. D. Lanier adopted the Greek Revival style of North Carolina when he constructed his Madison mansion. When the Civil War erupted, he advanced the State of Indiana more than a million dollars to finance the fighting.

J. F. D. LANIER HOUSE
MADISON, INDIANA

Banker's Mansion

By 1840, Midwestern architecture began to reflect the progress and prosperity which followed the Indian Wars of the first part of the century. A great influx of population from the Atlantic and Southern states brought with it a sophisticated cultural tradition which eventually replaced much of the primitive life of the early pioneers. Driving these people westward, agricultural interests had expanded, trade and manufacturing flourished and, most important, a revolution in transportation was underway. The waterways of the Midwest remained unchallenged by the burgeoning railroads during this period, but steam-propelled boats replaced barges and sail craft, providing easy access to the rich lands beyond the Allegheny Mountains.

In 1844, James F.D. Lanier, a well known and successful Indiana banker, built a home in Madison which was indicative of the new culture that emerged with rise of the Midwestern cities. Imported from his native North Carolina, the style of the colonnaded mansion was fashioned after the Greek Revival buildings which flourished in the East from 1820 to the time of the Civil War. The interior of the house is characterized by high ceilings, intricate moldings, and graceful columns which support exposed beams.

The nameplate of the architect, Francis Costigan, is embedded in the newel post of the mansion. Also a native of the East, Costigan was one of the first

---

J.F.D. Lanier State Memorial: Elm & W. First Streets, Madison, Indiana. Open to the public.

architect-builders to use pre-published blueprints. The house required a total of four years and $50,000 to build and was considered by Costigan to be his masterpiece.

Lanier had come to Madison with his parents when he was 17, later practicing law there and aiding in the creation of the Indiana State Bank. Nonetheless, he did not remain in the mansion beyond 1852. Drawn by the financial prospects of the East, he returned to New York where he amassed a personal fortune speculating in railroad securities. When the Civil War broke out, however, Lanier turned his attention toward Indiana once again. Despite a three per cent Federal income tax which was levied for the first time in 1861, the states had

to carry much of the burden of financing the war themselves. Indiana's Constitution of 1851 barred a state debt and its situation became desperate. Apparently, Lanier offered to finance the state's participation in the war. By the end of the conflict, he had advanced more than a million dollars.

Although he never returned to Madison after 1852, the Lanier House remained in the family until a son, Charles, presented it to the Jefferson County Historical Society. In 1925, the house was turned over to the State of Indiana, and has since been maintained as a period museum and a memorial to the man who came to the aid of Indiana during a crucial period in its history.

MARK TWAIN HOME

HANNIBAL, MISSOURI

Hannibal: Home of An American Original

The Mark Twain Home in Hannibal, Missouri, is known throughout the world as the Mississippi River home of Tom Sawyer in the fictional town of St. Petersburg. For it was here that an American original, Mark Twain (Samuel Langhorne Clemens), was raised and experienced many of the adventures which later produced the tales of Tom Sawyer and Huckleberry Finn.

The two-story frame house was built in 1844 by John Marshall Clemens, Sam's father, five years after he moved from Florida, Missouri, to open a general store. Sometime after the elder Clemens died in 1847, Sam's brother, Orion, moved his newpaper and printing shop into the house.

For awhile after this, young Sam worked for his brother on the newpaper, but his imagination and wit in print soon caused a separation. Leaving the newspaper to wander the country as a journeyman printer, he embarked on subsequent careers as a river pilot, miner, newspaper reporter, author and world celebrity. Of this separation, Orion later remarked, as he watched the newspaper move closer and closer to failure, "I could have distanced all

competitors even then if I had recognized Sam's ability and let him go ahead, merely keeping him from offending worthy persons."

It wasn't long after Sam's departure that the remainder of the Clemens family moved to Muscatine, Iowa, abandoning the house to an uncertain future in the market place until George A. Mahan, a lawyer and avid Mark Twain admirer, purchased it in 1912. Presenting the home intact to the town of Hannibal, and later contributing bronze statues of both Tom Sawyer and Huckleberry Finn, Mahan established the first of many memorials to Twain.

With the interior restored to its 19th-century appearance, the house at 206 Hill Street, is again the scene where young Sam Clemens administered pain killer to Peter the cat and escaped out of a second-story window to meet Tom Blankenship (later known as Huckleberry Finn) for a round of midnight pranks. Here also, his mother, his sister Pamela and brother Henry were later transformed into the characters of Aunt Polly, Mary and Sid. The board fence around the house which Sam Clemens, and later Tom Sawyer, duped neighbor-

Mark Twain Home: 208 Hill Street, Hannibal, Missouri. Open to the public.

hood boys into whitewashing for him is gone; but a duplicate now stands in its place.

Other landmarks in Hannibal which may be spotted in Twain's two memorable works include the Laura Hawkins House, which stands across the street from the Twain home. Sam Clemens' boyhood sweetheart lived here, followed later by Becky Thatcher who won the heart of Tom Sawyer. Holliday's Hill, known to Twain's adventurous characters as Cardiff Hill, still overlooks the Mississippi River and Jackson's Island from which the

youthful St. Petersburg pirates launched many a dangerous excursion.

Perhaps the most graphic reminder of Twain's boyhood, however, is the cave where Tom Sawyer and Becky Thatcher became lost, fearfully promising themselves to each other forever. For it is here, in the labyrinthine passages two miles south of Hannibal, that tourists retrace their own childhood steps, following the evasive spirit of youth captured by the immortal words of Samuel Langhorne Clemens.

OCTAGON HOUSE
Bygone House of Tomorrow
WATERTOWN, WISCONSIN

In 1848, Orson Squire Fowler, a widely traveled practitioner of phrenology, published a book entitled *A Home for All*, inspired by the octagon construction he had observed in parts of the East. For a brief period after that this architectural form flourished, but its impact was not fully realized until 1933 when architect George Fred Keck used it as a prototype for his "House of Tomorrow" at the Century of Progress Exposition at Chicago.

One of the most elaborate of the early octagon houses was built by John Richards in 1854 in Watertown, Wisconsin. This five-level, 57-room mansion is not only the best preserved example of this architectural form; it represents, as well, the inventiveness of its designer, with its systems of running water, air conditioning and central hot-air heating.

Richards, who was born in Massachusetts, came to Wisconsin in 1837. A successful lawyer and owner of at least two saw and grist mills, he designed and built the house with the intention of making it the largest in the State of Wisconsin. The first three floors were to be used for the family, the fourth for the mill workers and the fifth as a small observatory.

The floor plans for each of the first four stories are exactly alike. Four large square rooms surround

a circular, cantilever staircase which extends from the second to the fifth level. The partitioning of these rooms from the octagon base leaves four, correspondingly smaller, wedge-shaped spaces which were originally utilized as service areas and bedrooms. The fifth level consists of an octagonal glass enclosed cupola, set into the mansion's concave roof. This was designed to provide much of the light for the spiral staircase.

The outside walls, surrounded by a colonnaded porch, are 13 inches thick and constructed in a manner which enabled Richards to improvise a system of air conditioning and heating. Three separate walls were actually built, leaving a four-inch space between each layer of brick. When vents were placed in all of the partitions, there was a continuous circulation of fresh air from the outside while the triple-thickness of the walls insulated the house against the summer heat. Along with the vents, registers were installed throughout the interior partition. During the winter months, hot air was transmitted into the rooms through these vents from a wood-burning furnace on the first level. The concave roof above the fourth floor provided the source for the water system. A basswood tank, located on the

---

Octagon House: 919 Charles Street, Watertown, Wisconsin. Open to the public. Color illustration, p. 146.

Above: Years after the adventures which produced the characters of Tom Sawyer and Huckleberry Finn, Mark Twain returned to Hannibal, Missouri. Many of the landmarks which appear in Twain's two memorable works have been preserved .

third floor, received the rain water funneled from the roof, and passed it on by gravity to facilities in the lower levels of the house through lead pipes.

Succeeding generations of the Richards family occupied the house for 84 years before it was donated to the Watertown Historical Society in 1938. Left with most of the original furnishings intact, this house represents not only a passing architectural fancy but, as Keck wrote when he designed the House of Tomorrow, "To me the importance of the Octagon House lies in the inventive spirit the designer has displayed."

Right: The Octagon House has period pieces which contrast with its ingenious devices for running water, central heating and air conditioning. Owner-architect John Richards intended it to be the largest house in Wisconsin.

161

HULL HOUSE
CHICAGO, ILLINOIS

Reformer in Chicago

Jane Addams grew to maturity during the last years of the 19th century, when the rapid expansion of industry and transportation and a great influx in immigration produced severe slum conditions in most urban areas throughout the country. She was to become a potent force in combating those conditions and alleviating their unfortunate results.

The daughter of a well-to-do Quaker businessman and politician, she was raised in Cedarville, Illinois, which is about 120 miles northwest of Chicago. From her childhood, Jane Addams had been sick; curvature of the spine and the resulting weakness plagued her all her life.

In 1881, the year she graduated from Rockford Seminary, her father died. The shock of her father's death, together with an operation to correct the curvature and recovery from it, kept her in bed for almost a year. She did not completely recover from her state of nervous exhaustion for several years.

During this restless and unhappy period she traveled twice to Europe and these journeys seemed to help her to find the purpose in life that she was seeking. She became acutely aware of the poverty in Europe, and in Madrid, during the second trip (1887-1888), her ideas seemed to crystallize. After watching a bullfight, she became disgusted with her lack of reaction to the torture in the bullring and her years of thought without social action. Then and there she decided to open a settlement house for the underprivileged and she asked one of the women in the party with her in Madrid, Ellen Gates Starr, her friend from Rockford Seminary, to help her.

Before returning to America, she visited Toynbee Hall, an English settlement house, the first in the world, established to ease slum conditions there. Back in this country, she went to Chicago to begin her project, settling on the Charles J. Hull mansion as her headquarters several months later.

This house, built in 1856 and located in the heart of Chicago's sweatshop district, remained as a vestige of the prosperity achieved by Chicago residents prior to the Civil War. Hull, a wealthy real estate dealer, used it as his summer home. An adaption of Greek Revival design, the two-story

Hull House: Polk & Halsted Streets, Chicago, Illinois. Open to the public.

Below: When Jane Addams bought the Hull mansion for the first settlement house in this country, it was a vestige of antebellum prosperity in Chicago's sweatshop district. Her decision to open the house came at a Madrid bullfight.

University of Illinois

MIDWESTERN HOUSES

Right: Kentucky rifles hang over the mantel in the combination study, library and office of Governor Worthington. The tomahawk was given to him by the renowned Shawnee chief, Tecumseh, as a sincere token for his hospitality after a visit to the home in 1807.

Below: Adena, the Chillicothe country home of Ohio's sixth governor, Thomas Worthington, was planned by Benjamin Latrobe. The cut-stone mansion simulates the Georgian architecture so highly regarded by the refined and wealthy plantation owners of the South.

Above: A 16th-century rock crystal plaque entitled "Cupid Holding a Swan" typifies the variety and distinction of a collection in Cincinnati's Taft Museum whose pieces are representative of the major artistic flowerings of the French and Italian Renaissance.

Left: Joaquín Sorolla y Bastida's impressive portrait of William Howard Taft is part of an outstanding collection of important paintings tastefully arranged throughout the Taft mansion and including major works by Turner, Sargent and Rembrandt.

*Above: The former Taft home, now known as the
Taft Museum, was built along the expansive lines of
early Republican country houses in Virginia and Maryland.
It was from the front portico that William Howard
Taft accepted the 1908 Presidential nomination.*

Phil McCafferty

Above: Hercules Dousman, Wisconsin's first millionaire, chose Prairie du Chien as the site for the grand home he built in 1843. Unrivaled in its elegance, the house known as Villa Louis became an oasis of culture in a barely tame frontier.

Wisconsin Conservation Dept. by N. Barger, Jr.

Left: The bedroom of Louis Dousman at Villa Louis contains some exceptionally fine examples of mid-Victorian furnishings. Outstanding is the walnut bed with removable headboard. The portrait is that of Hercules Dousman II, the son of Villa Louis' builder.

(Continued from page 162)

mansion had a large portico which extended around three sides and was supported by tall Corinthian columns. Precisely turned gingerbread woodwork, which today still adorns doorways and windows, was produced by prison laborers.

Hull House officially opened a few months after Jane Addams returned from England. Its purpose was to stimulate social and cultural growth as well as to feed, clothe and help find jobs for the thousands of immigrant families. A kindergarten for the children of working mothers and an employment bureau were followed later by an art gallery, library and a music and crafts school. By the turn of the century, 12 additional buildings were incorporated into Hull House, including a theater, gymnasium, nursery, residents' dining hall and apartments for residents.

Among other projects launched by Jane Addams and her associates were the Immigrants' Protective League, the Juvenile Protective Association, the first city-operated playground, the Institute for Juvenile Research, the Illinois Child Labor Committees and the Juvenile Court. In 1893, after sponsoring the labor organizations of the shirt and cloak workers, Hull House efforts led to the enactment of the first state factory law, prohibiting the employment of children, fixing an eight-hour day for women and providing for factory inspectors.

Also in this year, Jane Addams secured the position of garbage inspector for Chicago, dramatizing her struggle for sanitation reform.

The heterogeneous population that surrounded Hull House emphasized the need for different nationalities to live peacefully together. Applying this concept to national affairs, Jane Addams joined the Women's Peace Party, taking an active role at the Hague in 1915. For her subsequent organization and leadership of the International Women's League for Peace and Freedom, in 1931 Jane Addams became the first woman to receive the Nobel Peace Prize.

By the time of her death in 1935, Hull House had become the driving force behind the Chicago Federation of Settlements and the National Federation of Settlements. The social work which began over 70 years ago in Hull House is being carried on today in Chicago by the Hull House Association in six different Chicago locations. Of the 13 buildings which became Hull House, only two are left: the original Charles Hull mansion (the first Hull House building) and the residents' dining hall. These two buildings in their original location, now the site of the new Circle Campus of the University of Illinois in Chicago, are a memorial to Jane Addams, to Hull House and to the residents who made it what it is today.

ULYSSES S. GRANT HOUSE
GALENA, ILLINOIS

Sam Grant's Galena Mansion

Ulysses S. Grant's arrival in Galena, Illinois, represented both the lowest ebb and the turning point of his career. The story is well known: An 1843 graduate of the U.S. Military Academy at West Point, Grant had achieved some distinction in the Mexican War but, subsequent to his retirement from the Army 11 years later, he failed successively at farming, auctioneering and account collecting. As a result, financial necessity drew him

to Galena during the first year of the Civil War, where he hired himself out as a clerk in his father's leather store.

Unknown either to "Sam" Grant or the leading citizens of Galena, the next four years would see them raising $16,000 in order to present him with one of the finest Victorian homes in the city.

The house, not far from the Galena River, was built by Alexander Jackson in 1859, as Galena, one

---

U.S. Grant House: Bouthillier Street, Galena, Illinois. Open to the public. Color illustration, p. 143.

of the first boom towns in America, approached the height of its prosperity. Designed after the Greek Revival style, the two-story brick residence with wide, overhanging eaves, represented the best mid-Victorian architecture of the period. The town itself was established during the 1820's when extensive lead deposits were discovered in the surrounding hills. In succeeding years, great personal fortunes were amassed from these mines, and river traffic soon made Galena a leading center of trade in the Midwest.

During the first months that Grant was in Galena, he lived obscurely in a small house overlooking much of the town. This house, along with the mansion and the leather store where he worked, is preserved today. When Galena volunteers organized as a unit for the Civil War, Grant became their drillmaster, accompanying the small company to Springfield, where he secured a commission as a colonel in the Illinois 21st Infantry Regiment. Within the next year following repeated military successes in Western campaigns, Grant was promoted to brigadier general. Two years later, when he was given command of all the armies of the United States by President Lincoln, he was promoted to lieutenant general.

After Lee's capitulation at Appomattox ended hostilities, a victorious General Grant returned to Galena where citizens had draped a banner across Main Street reading: "Hail to the Chief Who In Triumph Advances." At this time Grant accepted the presentation of the Jackson mansion and, according to a chronicle of the period, "showed his intention of making it his permanent home by bringing his war trophies with him."

Although Grant always considered the Galena home his legal residence, the period after the war until his death in 1885 allowed him little time there. In 1867 he assumed the duties of Secretary of War for a short time and became a leader in the postwar Reconstruction program. By 1868, he was the logical Republican choice for President.

Soon after he won the election, he left Galena for eight years in the White House. Returning to Illinois in 1879 from a tour around the world, he remained there until early 1880 when the Grants went to Mexico, never to return to Galena. Shortly thereafter he was defeated for renomination for President, and he moved to New York, where he spent his last days writing his *Personal Memoirs*.

Despite his apparent abandonment of the Galena mansion, the house remained in the family until 1904 when Frederick Dent Grant, the eldest son, deeded it to the City of Galena in memory of the general and former President. Some years later the house passed to the State of Illinois and, in 1955, a complete restoration was undertaken. Preservation of the original plans and specifications, drawn by Alexander Jackson in 1859, permitted authentic structural restoration and many of the original Grant furnishings were available for the interior. Among these, an old horsehair-covered parlor set is displayed on a new loop Brussels carpet, containing the same colors and exact pattern as the original. The Haviland china displayed in the dining room is that which was bought for Grant's daughter in 1874.

Of the nine Civil War generals who came from Galena, Ulysses S. Grant was by far the most prominent. As if cognizant of this fact, when the Grants left Galena for the last time in 1880, the town settled into a quiet decline from which it never recovered.

Illinois Dept. of Conservation

Above: Many of the pieces displayed in the ornately furnished Grant House at Galena, Illinois, are mementos from Grant's trip around the world after two terms as President. The vases on the mantel were a gift from the King of Bohemia.

Above: Handsome set on the table in the Grant dining room is part of the Haviland china bought for Grant's daughter in 1874. The Grants left Galena a few years after this, never to return, when Grant lost the Presidential nomination in 1880.

EISENHOWER FAMILY HOME

ABILENE, KANSAS

The General from Abilene

The boyhood home of General and former President Dwight David Eisenhower — now part of the Eisenhower Center at Abilene, Kansas — is a memorial to Eisenhower, and to the simple and vigorous family which produced this successful soldier and statesman. It was built in the 1880's by Eisenhow-er's grandfather, the Reverend Jacob Eisenhower, and is typical of the two-story, frame houses which were common throughout the Midwest at the time.

One of seven boys, Eisenhower was born in Denison, Texas, when his father became discouraged by an unsuccessful attempt to operate a

---

Eisenhower Family Home: S.E. Fourth Street, Abilene, Kansas. Open to the public.

Above: In his early years at Abilene, former President Eisenhower chanced to see a gun fight before the frontier was finally tamed. The house now belongs to the Eisenhower Museum, dedicated to servicemen and women of World War II.

general store and left Kansas for a job with the railroad. Two years later, however, in 1891, the Eisenhowers returned to the Abilene area, eventually buying the old frame house from an uncle who migrated West as an evangelist preacher. Eisenhower's father obtained work at the Belle Springs Creamery Plant where, years later, he became an engineer. Nonetheless, his salary never rose over $100 a month. Despite this apparent material lack, Eisenhower later recalled a "cheerful and vital family . . . with simple pleasures, but plenty of fresh air, exercise and companionship."

The forces that went into the fashioning of a general and President seem much the same as those that have prodded most boys out of infancy and into manhood. This family of eight squeezed into the 818 square feet of the two-story dwelling, and four of the boys occupied two double beds which nearly filled their one room. The tragedies that inevitably occurred simply because there were six boys about, ranged from Edgar's getting kicked by the horse one morning while cleaning the barn to an accident at play which blinded brother Earl in one eye.

Because of the limited resources of the family, the boys were each allotted a plot in the family garden where they could raise vegetables and sell

them for a profit. To supplement this activity, young "Ike," as he was called from childhood, sold Mexican hot tamales at a nickel-a-piece from a recipe his mother had obtained while they were in Texas. Although the chores of the garden kept all the boys busy during much of their leisure time, Ike still found occasion to fight with the other boys of the neighborhood, perform gravity-defying feats in the barn that never defied gravity, and even witness a gun fight before Abilene was completely transformed from a free-swinging Western town to a placid residential community.

His school days were spent with, perhaps, less concern for the future than would be usual today, but education didn't appear to be so important then. Undeclared holidays were generously consumed, for example, each year during the World Series as groups of truant boys huddled around the telegraph office, waiting for the baseball scores to be ticked off the miles of wire from an Eastern or Midwestern city.

Eisenhower's decision to attend a service academy after he left high school was partially derived from an earlier and continuing interest in military history, but the compelling factor was the decision of a friend to enroll in the Naval Academy at

Annapolis. The two boys took the exams, which applied to both West Point and Annapolis; but before the results were returned, Ike learned that he would be barred from enrollment in the Naval Academy because he would be nearly 21 before the start of the next session. As a result, he left for West Point in June 1911, having received top scores for entrance at either academy.

The years between his admission to West Point and the end of World War II brought Eisenhower to one of the heights of his military career and to the brink of political prominence, as well. Returning as a great world hero to his Abilene home from Europe in 1945, Eisenhower was greeted by his aging mother the year before her death. His father had died three years earlier. In 1947 the five surviving Eisenhower brothers, Arthur, Edgar, Dwight, Earl and Milton donated the house to the Eisenhower Foundation in Abilene, which has since given it to the United States as a shrine to all the men and women who served in the armed forces during World War II.

CARRY NATION HOUSE
MEDICINE LODGE, KANSAS
Battling Carry's First March

When Carry A. Nation moved into the one-story, yellow brick cottage which bears her name today, Medicine Lodge, Kansas, was a bristling, frontier cattle town. The house, built sometime during the 1870's, is an unimposing structure with a simple gabled roof and a small porch on the north side. It presented a striking contrast to the stout, unyielding woman who emerged from its protection one summer afternoon in 1899, launching her first violent crusade against what she considered the evils of the liquor traffic.

The daughter of a prosperous Irish slave trader and cattleman, Carry Nation was widowed and left with an ailing child at the age of 24, when her first husband died as the result of excessive drinking. Her second husband, David Nation, whom she married four years later, was a Union veteran, newspaper editor, lawyer and ordained minister. She accompanied him to Texas where he unsuccessfully engaged in hotel management and farming, finally moving to Medicine Lodge in 1889, when he was appointed minister of the Christian Church there.

One of her primary reasons for settling in Kansas was the existence of a statewide prohibition law in that state. Upon her arrival in Medicine Lodge, however, she was immediately faced with the prospect of seven saloons operating in flagrant violation of this law along the town's main street.

Through almost nine years, Carry Nation lived quietly, generously ministering to the needs of her husband's congregation, showing kindness toward anyone in need. But finally, on that summer afternoon toward the end of the decade, she led a small group of women to one of the saloons, at first content to lead them in singing a few hymns outside the swinging, front doors. Then, armed only with a stout umbrella, she advanced with her modest group to destroy the interior of the building. A short but vigorous struggle ended when she and her band were forcefully expelled from the saloon; but their persistent singing for the remainder of the afternoon forced the proprietor to close early. The next day he left town. Encouraged by this success, Carry Nation organized other women in Medicine Lodge who had suffered at the hands of drinking husbands and launched a scathing attack against town officials who condoned these law violations.

A year later, having eliminated the saloons in

Carry Nation House: U.S. Route 160, Medicine Lodge, Kansas. Open to the public.

Medicine Lodge, Carry Nation moved on to the neighboring town of Kiowa where, singlehandedly, she nearly obliterated one establishment with rocks wrapped in newspaper. Militantly referring to herself as the "John Brown of Prohibition," she traveled next to Wichita, at the time the second largest city in Kansas. It was here that she first wielded the hatchet with which she was identified throughout the rest of her years of anti-saloon campaigning.

In the last years of her short career, she traveled widely, lecturing throughout the United States and England and extending her campaign far beyond the limits of prohibition. Some of her more vehement critics have even accused her of "meddling with people's lovemaking and the length of women's skirts."

Today, located on its original site at the west end of the Medicine Lodge Stockade, the Carry Nation house is preserved as a museum, maintaining the simple décor and furnishings as they were before the turn of the century — before this hatchet-wielding priestess of hellfire and brimstone began a career which inspired more love and hatred and — in the long run — legislation than any other woman of her time.

Below: The Carry Nation House at Medicine Lodge, Kansas, appears incongruously peaceful as it was rendered by a contemporary artist more than a half-century after the fiery prohibitionist put down her hatchet and Bible for the last time.

HERBERT HOOVER BIRTHPLACE COTTAGE

WEST BRANCH, IOWA

A President's Iowa Boyhood

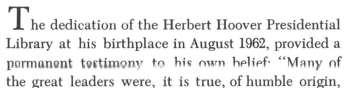

The dedication of the Herbert Hoover Presidential Library at his birthplace in August 1962, provided a permanent testimony to his own belief: "Many of the great leaders were, it is true, of humble origin, but that alone was not their greatness."

The two-room cottage in West Branch, Iowa — on which restoration work was begun in 1938 and opened to visitors the following year — was built around 1870 by Hoover's father, Jesse Clark Hoover, a Quaker blacksmith. Here, four years later, "Bert," as he was affectionately nicknamed, was born the second of three children and spent his first years.

Many years later Hoover wrote in his memoirs: "I prefer to think of Iowa as I saw it through the eyes of a ten-year-old boy — and the eyes of all ten-year-old Iowa boys are or should be filled with the wonders of Iowa's streams and woods, of the mystery of growing crops. His days should be filled with adventure and great undertaking, with participation in good and comforting things."

One of Hoover's "bitterest days" in Iowa was in connection with a rabbit he and his older brother had trapped. They wanted to bring it home alive because as Hoover said, "in the lore of boys of my time," it was better to do so. But rabbits fresh from the trap on a cold morning are "wiggly rabbits," so Hoover's brother instructed him "to hold up the rabbit by its hind feet while with his not over-sharp knife he proposed to puncture two holes between the sinews and back knee joints of the rabbit, through which holes he proposed to tie a string and thus arrive at complete security. Upon the introduction of the operation the resistance of this rabbit was too much for me. I was not only blamed for its escape all the way home and for weeks afterwards, but continuously over the last 40 years."

When Hoover was ten years old his mother died of pneumonia, following her husband who had suffered the same death four years earlier. The three Hoover children were separated and sent to live with various Iowa relatives. A year later, Herbert journeyed to Oregon to live with an uncle. At 17, outfitted with two suits and a bicycle, Hoover left Oregon for Palo Alto, California, where he received a Bachelor of Arts degree in geology with the first graduating class at Stanford University in 1895. Two years later, he accepted a position with an Australian mining firm.

He circled the globe five times before World War I, one of his more exciting experiences taking place around the turn of the century. Hoover was working at the head of the Chinese Engineering and Mining Company in Tientsin, China, when he and his bride were trapped as the Boxer Rebellion erupted. It was during the few violent months of this revolt that Hoover had his first experience with war and refugees that led him in succeeding years to become one of the world's outstanding humanitarians.

When hostilities broke out in 1914, Hoover was asked by the United States Ambassador to England and others, to organize and direct the American Relief Committee which led ultimately to the creation of the Commission for Relief in Belgium under his charge. At the height of this work, Hoover was directing food supplies for over 250 million people in 22 different nations. Similar work was carried on by Hoover in Russia during a famine in the early 1920's and again at the conclusion of World War II he brought relief to Europe. Flour sacks which hang in the Herbert Hoover Presidential Library, also located at West Branch were returned to Hoover by many grateful Europeans, embroidered with expressions of their gratitude.

Altogether, Hoover served in the cabinets or headed commissions of five Presidents, serving four years in the Presidency, himself. During his single

Herbert Hoover Birth place Cottage: West Branch, Iowa. Open to the public. Color illustration, p. 145.

term in office, his administration was responsible for, among other things, reforms of the criminal procedure for Federal courts and organization of the Federal Bureau of Investigation as an effective agency. With the crash of the stock market in October, 1929, however, the country was immersed in panic. Despite Hoover's unprecedented attempts to stabilize the national economy, the fear and uncertainty which prevailed in almost all quarters of American life signaled the end of his political career.

Following his defeat in 1932, Hoover remained out of politics throughout the Roosevelt Administration except to issue periodic warnings to the American people at large about what he believed to be the indiscriminate surrender of freedom as Government control increased. Focusing the major portion of his attention through these years on projects which had been started prior to and during

his term as President, he participated in the raising of $50,000,000 to $75,000,000 over the next 15 years for charitable undertakings. During the last years of his life, however, Hoover was called back into public service in both the Truman and Eisenhower administrations where he continued his humanitarian endeavors and headed two commissions seeking ways to improve the organization of the executive branch of the Government.

In 1955 Hoover finished his work with the commissions and retired from public life to write a history of the 20th century as he saw it and made it. Nine years later he died, leaving in his works and writings only a partial indication of things he transported with him back to that humble origin above the Wapsinonoc Creek at West Branch, Iowa, where he is buried.

MELLETTE HOUSE
WATERTOWN, SOUTH DAKOTA

South Dakota's Struggle for Statehood

Arthur C. Mellette was the last Governor of the Dakota Territory and the first Governor of South Dakota when it achieved statehood in 1890. A successful lawyer, newspaperman and politician in his native Indiana, Mellette moved to the Dakota Territory in 1778 because of his wife's failing health. Two years later, as registrar of the U.S. Land Office, he settled in Watertown when the office was transferred there from Springfield. By this time, sentiment among citizens in the lower portion of the territory for statehood and entrance into the Union was growing intense.

In 1885 Mellette was elected chairman of a convention to consider statehood for the territory below the 46th parallel. Early the next year, a constitution was completed and forwarded to Washington for approval. Mellette put $16,000 of his own money into the campaign for statehood during

this time, but little was accomplished until 1889 when President Benjamin Harrison appointed Mellette territorial governor. The following year, South Dakota was admitted to the Union and Mellette embarked on a three-year term as the first governor of the state.

In 1883 he built the house which is memorialized now on Mellette Hill in Watertown. This two-story, red brick building, with its wide overhanging eaves and balustraded porticos, is a fine example of mid-Victorian architecture. Mellette, however, lived in the house for only a little over ten years. At the end of his term as as governor in 1893, it was discovered that his state treasurer, W.W. Taylor, had absconded with $350,000 in public funds. Although it was not Mellette's personal responsibility, he put his house and possessions against the debt before he left office. Two years

---

Mellette House: 421 Fifth Avenue, Watertown, South Dakota. Open to the public.

later, his great personal fortune dissipated, Mellette journeyed from Watertown to Pittsburg, Kansas, where he died in 1896 attempting to revive his neglected law practice.

Years later, the state legislature returned the house to Mrs. Mellette, but it passed out of her hands soon afterward and was allowed to deteriorate until the formation of the Mellette Memorial Association in 1946. This organization bought the house for $500, restored the building and secured most of the original furniture from Mellette's last surviving son who was then 96 years old.

Included in the articles now on display there is a volume of newspaper clippings, saved by the former governor, which depict his years of prominence in South Dakota politics. This memento, alone, is a priceless remembrance in the house of a man who spent a lifetime, a fortune and his own honor to pioneer and maintain the public image of statehood at a time when political power was highly suspect to tyranny in some quarters.

Below: South Dakota's first governor, Arthur C. Mellette, lost his home on Mellette Hill when he offered it as payment against a $350,000 embezzlement committed by his state treasurer. His fortune gone, he died a few years later in Kansas.

V WESTERN HOUSES

PALACE OF THE GOVERNORS
SANTA FE, NEW MEXICO

350 Years of Southwestern History

The 350-year-old Palace of the Governors marked the original settlement of Santa Fe when it became the capital of the Province of New Mexico in the Viceroyalty of New Spain in 1610. Probably completed the same year, the palace is the oldest surviving public building within the continental United States, having housed a total of six different governments. Aside from occupancy by the various heads-of-state who guided New Mexico from the time it was a Spanish possession to within a dozen years of its admission to the Union as a state in 1912, this includes a 12-year tenure by the Pueblo Indians when they revolted in 1680 and a brief occupation by the Confederate Army of the United States during the Civil War.

Initially, the palace was constructed on a ten-acre tract of land around an expansive courtyard. Within this framework, the governor established his quarters, as well as apartments for other government officials, servants' quarters, military barracks and stables. The east and west ends of the sprawling defense structures were reinforced with large observation towers similar in use and design to blockhouses. The east tower doubled as a chapel for the early Spaniards.

The first definite reference to the Palace of the Governors dates to the Indian revolt in 1680. During this year, the long-suffering Pueblo Indians besieged the fortified buildings, toppling the Spanish Government and burning official documents. As a result, the only proof of the structure's age is the construction order, dated March 1609, in the Archives of the Indies in Seville, Spain.

Forced out of the Santa Fe settlement, the surviving Spaniards retreated to the south, where they remained for 12 years, settling at the present-day site of Juárez, Mexico, across the Rio Grande from what is now El Paso, Texas. In 1692, however, Don Diego de Vargas reoccupied Santa Fe, once again establishing Spanish rule, and setting himself up as governor. He retained his army in the years following as an occupation force and constructed two rows of barracks which extended from the west wall of the palace. Years later, when Sante Fe had become a United States' city, these were removed.

During the absence of the Spanish, some

The Palace of the Governors: Palace Avenue, Santa Fe, New Mexico. Open to the public.

Above: The adobe-styled Palace of the Governors embraces nearly 300 years as a governmental headquarters. Below: The reception room in the palace, taken from an 1893 photo while L. B. Prince was governor, catches a young constituent napping.

changes were wrought in the adobe brick buildings. Puddled adobe portions, which remain today, reflect the Pueblo occupation there. They added several stories to the original structure and increased the number of defense towers from two to four. Few of these additions endured the successors of de Vargas, however, and in the years prior to the U.S. occupation, the entire palace complex deteriorated.

All the blood and toil which Spain had put into its New World empire came to nothing with the success of revolution in Mexico in 1821. With the end of Spanish commercial restrictions, William Becknell left Franklin, Missouri, in 1822 on his second trading mission to Santa Fe. Within a few years enough others followed his path to establish the first great Western trail — the Santa Fe.

With the independence from Spanish dictatorship and the increase in trade, Santa Fe changed and so did the tone of the palace. During the Mexican period, from 1821 to 1846, several legislative and advisory bodies met in the palace, which in 1837 was renamed the Council Hall for a time.

In August 1846, General Stephen Kearny took possession of the province for the United States, and the first session of the Territorial House of Representatives met in the palace four years later when New Mexico officially became a territory.

Under United States' control at this time, any of the outbuildings which had fallen into a state of disrepair were torn down and rebuilt. The east end of the palace, which had contained one of the massive observation towers, was reconstructed to house the new legislature and library; and in 1878, a front portal of peeled logs, supporting a dirt roof, was replaced by a balustrated Victorian porch. This last addition, however, was dismantled in 1913 in favor of a reproduction of the original.

In 1900, after 290 years as the seat of various governments, another building was designated as the capitol for the territorial government. Nine years later the Palace of the Governors was redesignated as the Museum of New Mexico; and in 1961, the Federal Government established the building and grounds as a National Historic Landmark.

SPANISH GOVERNORS' PALACE
SAN ANTONIO, TEXAS

Texas Heritage

The Governors' Palace was established in the mid-18th century at San Antonio de Bexar, as it was then called, well after Spanish influence was entrenched in Mexico and further exploration brought the Old World soldiers into the wilderness north of the Rio Grande River. At first the building served only as a fort; but when Texas was incorporated into the Spanish province of Mexico, the capital was designated at San Antonio and the fort, of which only the palace survives today, became the residence and headquarters for a long succession of governors.

Facing historic Military Plaza, the palace is constructed largely of stone with a plaster finish and has the long, low silhouette that is typical of Southwestern adobe architecture. The lower windows are reinforced with metal gratings, and massive hand-hewn beams jut through the three-foot-thick walls, supporting a flat gravel roof, also several feet in depth. The grounds are resplendent with gardens and shrubbery, through which a walk layed in light and dark colored pebbles leads to a fountain in the palace courtyard. Massive, paneled doors hang in the stone archway of the main entrance and depict, through beautifully elaborate carvings, Spain's discovery and conquest of Mexico and the Texas territory. The keystone over the main entrance doors bears the date 1749 and the Hapsburg coat of arms.

The beams, which extend through the outside walls, are exposed against the high ceilings of the interior, which is also finished in plaster. Most of

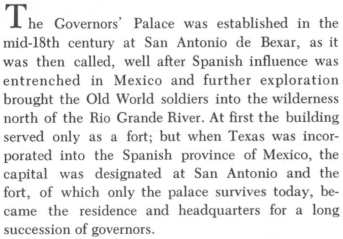

Spanish Governors' Palace: Military Plaza, San Antonio, Texas. Open to the public.

the floors throughout the ten rooms of the building are quarried blocks of stone or inlaid flagstones, but tiles baked in crude ovens have also survived.

Antique furnishings represent two distinct periods and types. Roughly fashioned benches and tables from the period when the palace was a military outpost exist alongside the handcrafted pieces imported by later governors, which represent some of the finest 17th-century Spanish designs. A turned rosewood bed with a grilled headpiece and carved pillars is typical of the heavy, ornate furnishings throughout the house, Illumination was provided by decorative chandeliers which hang from the exposed beams in each of the rooms.

In 1820, nearly 100 years after the building of the palace, a Missourian, Moses Austin, met with some Mexican officials in the ballroom, contracting an American settlement in Texas. A statue now stands in his honor in front of city hall across from the palace. The following year Mexico won her independence from Spain and Texas came under the jurisdiction of the newly formed republic.

The last Spanish governor to occupy the Governors' Palace was Antonio Martínez who was there from 1817 until 1821.

At first the newly independent Mexican government encouraged colonization of Texas by people from the United States and Europe, and the new settlers pledged their allegiance to Mexico. However, a new and dictatorial president, Santa Anna, inflicted severe hardships on the northern colony which culminated in the arrest of Stephen F. Austin, Moses Austin's son. When Austin was released in 1935 after two years as a prisoner, fighting soon erupted and the Texans declared their independence the following year.

Because it was a focal point of so much early Southwestern history, the Spanish Governors' Palace has attained a prominent position in the heritage of this country. Purchased in later years by the City of San Antonio to preserve a bit of this colorful history, the old palace stands now as a symbol of the aspirations and struggles of the Spanish north of the Rio Grande.

California Historical Society

Above: The rosewood bed in the office-bedroom of the Spanish Governors' Palace was imported during Spain's colonial era. Right: El Molino Viejo provided meal for over 4,000 Indians at the height of the Spanish Mission period.

EL MOLINO VIEJO
SAN MARINO, CALIFORNIA

Queen of the Missions Grist Mill

El Molino Viejo is among the last surviving buildings constructed in California by the Spanish before their expulsion, following the Mexican revolt for independence in 1821. Conceded to be the first water-powered grist mill in California, El Molino Viejo was built by Father José Maria de Zalvidea between 1810 and 1816, during his 20-year sovereignty at the San Gabriel Mission. At the height of the Spanish influence in California, El Molino Viejo provided ground meal for over 4,000 Indians of the San Gabriel Mission, known eventually as the "Queen of the Missions" because of its substantial prosperity.

The mission, founded in 1771, was the fourth to be built by the Spaniards as they penetrated northward from Mexico. Under the Spanish colonial system, these missions existed as outposts, through which the Spanish government instilled a loyalty to the crown in indigenous populations. The San Gabriel Mission was situated about nine miles east of present day Los Angeles at a point where trails from Mexico and the east converged, which made it a more popular site than many of the other missions. Also adding to San Gabriel's distinctive character was the mission church which, unlike the other colonial Spanish churches in California, traced its origin directly to Spain. Its architect, Father Antonio Crusado, received his early training at the cathedral of Cordova in Spain and later applied its Moorish design when he built the mission church at San Gabriel.

The old grist mill is a stout building with walls tapering from a five-foot thickness at the base to three feet near the tiled roof, the timbered beams for which were cut from the San Gabriel Mountains. The lower walls, plus the foundation, were quarried from veins of volcanic rock, while the upper walls and arched water chamber which fed the water wheels were fashioned from handmade bricks of fired adobe. Cement and limestone plaster used in the construction of the building were obtained from burning stone and sea shells respectively.

In building the mill, Father Zalvidea pioneered the use of the horizontal, direct impulse water wheel. Cement troughs carried water from the Kewen and Los Robles Canyons into storage cisterns along the west wall. A narrow spout flume at the bottom of the cistern transmitted the water into the arched water chamber, delivering it horizontally against the buckets of the water wheel. A vertical shaft extended through the center of the water wheel and joined the mill stone in the second story of the building, causing it to turn. However, the initial release of the water against the wheel did not provide enough force to set the large mill stone in motion. As a result, a group of Indians would begin the process by rapidly unwinding a leather thong wrapped about the shaft. Originally, a chamber supplied the wheel with water, but the earthquake of 1812 caused a large crack in one of the cisterns and it was never repaired.

El Molino Viejo was used only a few years before it was abandoned as a grist mill. Water spiraled up the turning shaft onto the mill stone and dampened the grain, making it impractical to store the meal there. A second mill was constructed opposite the mission in 1822, but nothing of that remains today. The death knell for El Molino Viejo as part of the San Gabriel Mission, however, was tolled in 1833 when the Mexican government confiscated the holdings of the Franciscan missionaries through the Secularization Act. From this time, the vast lands which had been a part of the mission, stretching from the mountains to the sea and from Los Angeles to San Bernardino, passed into private hands.

The first legal title holder to the property fol-

El Molino Viejo: 1120 Old Mill Road, San Marino, California. Open to the public.

lowing the Mexican era was Dr. Thomas White who, in 1858, deeded the property to his daughter, Fannie Kewen, for the sum of one dollar and his "natural love and affection." During the 20-year ownership of the Kewens, French doors, a fireplace and a front portico were added as the old grist mill was transformed into a private residence.

After Mr. Kewen's death, the property for which Doctor White had paid $500 was sold for $36,000. Succeeding owners utilized the building and grounds for a golf course and club house, a hotel and even a ranch; and it wasn't until early in the 20th century when its last owner remodeled the building, still as a private residence, that El Molino Viejo again approached its original appearance.

In 1962 it was deeded to the City of San Marino, which now maintains the mill as the Southern Quarters of the California Historical Society and as a memorial, not only to the historical era it represents, but to the inventiveness of the man who designed it and gave it the enduring qualities which have kept it intact until the present.

ADOBE COVARRUBIAS

SANTA BARBARA, CALIFORNIA

From Empire to Free State

Adobe Covarrubias is deeply rooted in the turbulent history that brought California out of the Spanish Empire, through the years of Mexican independence and into the United States. It was built in 1817 by Domingo Antonio Ignacio Carrillo, third son of Raimundo Carrillo, the commandant of the Santa Barbara Presidio. It is an unimposing structure, a single story surrounded by mounds of cactus, but its Spanish origin is unmistakable. The walls were constructed of sun-dried adobe brick securely buttressed with wedges of the same material. Unlike the American-built houses of this period and design, Adobe Covarrubias has a gently sloping roof supported by evenly cut timbers and neatly layed with red tile. The flagstone verranda, which begins under the protection of the extended roof, stretches out to a courtyard or patio, which is adorned with a fountain and small garden.

Carrillo was born at the San Diego Presidio in 1791, beginning his military career as a cadet there. In 1810, however, he married Concepción Pico and left the service several years later to build the house at Santa Barbara. In the years following, California was the scene of considerable violence and upheaval as Mexico wrenched her independence from Spain and established a succession of unstable territorial governments. Carillo re-entered the army, achieving the rank of lieutenant at Parisma in 1834. Two years later he became the commandant of the Santa Barbara Presidio at about the same time as the revolutionary Governor Alvarado declared California's independence from Mexico. This freedom was short-lived, however, as Alvarado submitted to the Mexican government and became the officially appointed provincial head. Carrillo had apparently failed to support either the revolutionary government or the reinstated body of the Mexicans and was subsequently discharged at Santa Barbara. A year later, in 1837, he died, leaving his wife and eight children.

The marriage of Carrillo's fifth child in 1838 to a French immigrant, José Maria Covarrubias, brought that name to the adobe dwelling. He was appointed secretary of the Department of California by Carrillo's brother-in-law, governor at the time of the Bear Flag Revolt of 1846 and Frémont's subsequent raising of the American flag at Monterey.

Despite his appointment as a Mexican official, Covarrubias did not oppose the American occupation and, after the annexation of California, he was elected as a delegate to the 1849 Constitutional Convention. One of the three original copies of that constitution remains now in the Santa Barbara

Adobe Covarrubias: 715 Santa Barbara St., Santa Barbara, Cal. Open to the public. Color illustration, p. 184

Historical Museum.

Following his attendance at the state convention, Covarrubias was elected to four terms in the general assembly and was holding that position when California was admitted to the Union a year later. In 1853 he became one of California's first Presidential electors, casting his vote for Franklin Pierce, and in 1861 he was elected a county judge. Throughout his lengthy career as a public official, he maintained his residence at the adobe where he died in 1870 at the age of 61.

Adobe Covarrubias endured a succession of owners during the next 100 years when, in 1964, it was purchased by the Santa Barbara Historical Society. Restored and furnished after the Covarrubias period, this modest adobe structure represents an extension of the Spanish Mission era in California, without which that nation's heritage in the New World would have crumbled and disappeared soon after the accession of Mexican independence.

FERNALD HOUSE

SANTA BARBARA, CALIFORNIA

The Law and the Vigilantes

Charles Fernald built his 14-room Santa Barbara house early in the 1860's, a decade after he was appointed sheriff there to restore law and order in the wake of the mounting lawlessness which followed the gold rush of 1849. In many areas of the state any semblance of civil rule had been replaced by vigilante committees and "lynch law." At the time of his appointment, Judge Fernald was passing through Santa Barbara on his way back to his native New England. Conditions in California had degenerated to such a point that most local officials were intimidated into resignation, and he was persuaded by friends to accept the position in order to try to eliminate the bands of marauders that terrorized the townspeople.

Fernald first came to California when he was 19, arriving in San Francisco in 1849 at the height of the gold rush. For awhile he worked in various mining camps, but soon returned to San Francisco where he worked on two newspapers and took up the serious study of law. It was three years later that he became Sheriff of Santa Barbara. Remaining there after law had been established, Fernald became the district attorney and was elected to three consecutive terms as county judge.

Finally, in 1862, he returned to North Berwick, Maine, where he was born in 1830. There he married Hannah Hobbs, by whom he had five children, returning to Santa Barbara during the same year to build a house for his new bride. The gabled roofs, the colonnaded front portico, and the upper balcony were all derivatives of his Eastern background, representing a definite departure from the Spanish architectural tradition that had grown up along the southwestern Pacific coast. The interior of the house was lavishly and ornately furnished, many of the pieces being handcrafted from solid redwood and remaining today, but even here there were signs of his New England associations.

In 1881 Judge Fernald was elected Mayor of Santa Barbara, while he continued his active law practice. During this period he was also admitted to practice in the State of California Supreme Court and the Supreme Court of the United States.

The house remained in the Fernald family a total of 96 years, passing to the Santa Barbara Historical Society in 1958 upon the death of Fernald's last surviving child. The will stipulated that the house be moved from its original location at 422 Santa Barbara Street where it had stood for nearly 100 years. This was accomplished by the society in 1959, at which time the house was restored to its original appearance and opened to the public.

A vestige of California's colorful history, the house now stands as a monument to the benefactors of law and justice throughout the country, reminding all men of the difficulty in achieving law before they would attempt to destroy it.

Fernald House: 412 W. Montecito St., Santa Barbara, Cal. Open to the public. Color illustration, p. 184.

WESTERN HOUSES

*Above: Larkin House in Monterey, California,
combines Spanish colonial and New England features.
The two-story adobe structure, constructed between 1834
and 1838, was the home of Thomas Larkin, California's
only United States consul to Mexico.*

Above: The construction of the venerable Adobe Covarrubias in Santa Barbara, California, during the Mission period, and the "river of life" pattern carved into its solid oak doors, indicate it was probably built by Indian labor.

Right: A handmade oak bed stands in the Fernald House in Santa Barbara, California. Judge Charles Fernald built and furnished a new home for his bride in 1867, and the house still remains as an example of Western pioneer living in the mid-19th century.

Left: Clothing of the 1890's is displayed at the Healy House State Historical Monument. Rich furnishings and ornamentation reflect the ease of manner and Old World graciousness characteristic of the good life during the Gay Nineties.

Below: August Meyer's choice for the site of his Leadville, Colorado, dwelling was greatly influenced by the beauty of the Western range. His home, now known as Healy House, faced the Great Divide, and gave an air of tradition to its surroundings.

Left: The primitive but cheerful kitchen of the Kit Carson Home in Taos, New Mexico, has a large bell-shaped cooking fireplace built into the corner of the room, a feature of the nearby Taos Indian Pueblos which was copied by the colonists.

Below: The lavish Bowers Mansion in Washoe County, Nevada, was a dream come true for Sandy and Eilley Orrum Bowers who struck it rich with the Comstock Lode. Mrs. Bowers' private rooms, including her bedroom, have been restored with the original furnishings.

KIT CARSON HOME
TAOS, NEW MEXICO

House of a Hero

When Kit Carson bought this 12-room, adobe house for his Spanish bride in 1843, his reputation as an Indian fighter and frontiersman was already well established. He would become even more prominent for his exploits of heroism during the Mexican and Civil Wars, but this house would be Carson's permanent residence until he died 25 years later. He would be away from Taos much of the time during those years, but six and probably seven of his eight children were born there and seven of his more rewarding as well as frustrating years would be spent there as Indian agent.

Constructed in 1825 by an unidentified owner, the house is a single-story affair, designed in stockade fashion around a central patio or garden. Peculiar in its construction were the different levels of each of the rooms, caused by raising the walls of the house first and then packing the dirt floors to the easiest accessible level in each room. Until a saw mill was available in the 1860's the dirt floors were retained throughout the house. The exterior walls of the building were constructed from adobe brick, reaching a thickness of 30 inches, and covered with an adobe plaster material. Exposed ceiling beams of peeled logs jutted through this outer wall and supported a dirt roof also several feet thick. To provide heat and cooking facilities, fireplaces were built into practically every room.

Today, three of the rooms have been restored, using many of the original furnishings, to reflect a living room, kitchen and bedroom of the Carson era. The remainder of the rooms, not used for administrative purposes, contain collections of articles which provide a commentary on the different periods of Carson's life. In all, there are five such display areas — the Carson Room, Early American Room, Spanish Room, Indian Room and Chapel.

At the conclusion of the Mexican War in 1848, Carson returned to Taos from his government assignment of carrying dispatches from Los Angeles to Washington, D.C. He was greeted by news of the merciless slaughter of his brother-in-law, the territorial governor, during an Indian uprising. This was neither the first nor the last uprising which was to occur in the Southwest, nor would it be the only treaty between the Indians and the United States' Government to be violated. However, when Carson was appointed Indian agent in 1853, a period of relative peace followed, during which he traced the source of the trouble in several reports to his superiors — hunger and poverty. The Indians had been removed from their lands to make way for the white settlers. They had been promised monetary grants, food and clothing in return for accepting the restricted reservation life; and when these things were not forthcoming they revolted. Although Carson led several expeditions against the Indians himself he continually asserted that they be governed with the same integrity afforded the majority of the American people so they would eventually realize the "power and privilege of being an American." Throughout his years as Indian agent, these pleas fell on deaf ears. Nonetheless, he maintained his position, declaring a few days before his death that "all Indian trouble was originated by bad white men...that the bad Indians were trying to imitate the bad whites."

After 1868, the Carson house passed through no less than six owners when, in 1910, it was purchased and restored by the Masonic Lodge of Taos. It wasn't until 1952, however, that the Kit Carson Memorial Foundation was established and the house opened to the public. Now adjacent to the 19-acre Kit Carson Memorial State Park, the house remains as a monument to an early frontiersman who sought peace through justice.

Kit Carson Home and Museum: E. Kit Carson Ave., Taos, New Mexico. Open to the public. Color illustration, p. 186.

THOMAS O. LARKIN HOUSE
MONTEREY, CALIFORNIA

The Days of the Bear Flag Revolt

Some weeks after the Bear Flag Revolt of 1846, in which a handful of poorly equipped Californians attempted to secure freedom from Mexico, the Thomas Oliver Larkin House became the first (*de facto*) United States capitol in that state. Because of his close association with Mexican officials through his business interests, Larkin had been appointed American consul there three years earlier and was charged with promoting President James K. Polk's plans for a peaceful annexation of California. By 1846, however, Larkin's mission had proven largely unnecessary.

Even before the citizens' revolt, fighting had erupted between American and Mexican forces along the Rio Grande, and hostilities soon expanded to include California as well. On July 7 of the same year, the United States Naval Commander, Commodore John D. Sloat, put a force ashore at Monterey and raised the American flag. This incident was followed in 1848 by the negotiation of the Guadalupe Hidalgo Treaty, in which Mexico recognized the Rio Grande River as her northern boundary, surrendering her provinces of New Mexico and California and all the territory which lay between.

Larkin was originally from New England, born at Charleston, Massachusetts, in 1802 and orphaned at the age of 16. For nearly 15 years thereafter, he worked at several jobs around Boston and operated businesses in both North and South Carolina. In 1832, after a year at sea, he arrived at Monterey, California, where he prospered in lumber and grist mills. During the years preceding the Mexican War, he expanded his activities to include an active trade with Mexico and the Sandwich Islands for flour, soap, pelts, lumber, potatoes and horses.

Entering the mercantile business, Larkin and his partner became the leading Monterey merchants. Always industrious, he visited Mexico in 1840 and became friends with many leading citizens there.

During the years of conflict which preceded California's independence from Mexico, Larkin conferred with a number of important military figures at his Monterey residence. Among them were General Stephen W. Kearny, who would become California's governor for a brief period in 1847 and Lieutenant William T. Sherman. Promoted to general in the years following, Sherman was destined to lead the famous march from Atlanta to the sea during the Civil War, in which a 60-mile swath of devastation was cut across Georgia.

At one time during the struggle with Mexico, Larkin was held captive for a brief period by the Californians, but after his release he was instrumental in the writing of the California State Constitution in 1849. Larkin left the Monterey residence in 1850, living for awhile on the East Coast. He returned to California, however, before the end of the decade and settled in San Francisco where he died of typhoid fever in 1858.

The two-story, adobe building, which also served briefly as the American consulate, became the pattern for the Monterey style of architecture. The gently sloping, hipped roof was covered with redwood shingles and extended beyond the building on all four sides. Beneath this, a railed portico encompassed the second story, forming a cover for the ground-level verranda. The interior of the house with its wide-plank floors was finished with plaster and, unlike many other buildings of the era, concealed the heavy ceiling beams which supported the roof. The furnishings, a few of which remain today, were a combination of New England colonial and Southern plantation designs.

In the 60 years which followed Larkin's death, the house passed through only two owners, returning to the family when it was purchased by Mrs. Henry W. Toulmin, Larkin's granddaughter, in 1922. She carried out minor repairs and main-

Thomas O. Larkin House: Jefferson &. Calle Principal, Monterey, Calif. Open to the public. Color illustration, p. 183.

tenance and presented the house to the State of California in 1957. Preserved now as a California State Historical Monument, the Thomas O. Larkin House represents an important segment of Califor-nia history and, in its architecture, a significant departure from the Spanish influence along the southern Pacific coast.

THE MURRELL HOUSE
TAHLEQUAH (PARK HILL), OKLAHOMA

Cherokee Days in Oklahoma

In 1830, President Andrew Jackson was vigorously pursuing his policy of Indian removal from the Southeastern states. During the winter of that year, the Cherokee nation which had prospered through Tennessee and Georgia was dispossessed. They were moved to the Indian Territory which is now Oklahoma. The first of these newly arrived settlers established themselves at Park Hill and Tahlequah, where they continued their prosperity. Tahlequah became the new capital of the Cherokees and is considered the oldest incorporated city in Oklahoma.

Prior to the Indian migration, a Virginian by the name of George Michael Murrell married Minerva Ross, daughter of the Cherokee tribal treasurer and niece of its chief. In 1840 Murrell and his Indian bride arrived at the Park Hill settlement where they were provided with a modest log cabin as a gift from the tribal leaders. Murrell began a dry goods store and later opened a branch at neighboring Tahlequah where he became the city's first postmaster in 1847. His store was the first brick building to be constructed at Tahlequah.

The Cherokees made a concerted effort to educate themselves in their new surroundings and promote a prosperous, cultural society. Within a few years after their migration from the east, over the "Trail of Tears," the Cherokees established two institutions for higher learning. The Cherokee Male and Female Seminaries were erected at costs approaching $60,000 each.

Even before President Jackson issued the final removal order, the handful of Indians who had already settled in Oklahoma were reading many classical and religious texts printed at the Park Hill Press. Further evidence of the progress realized in the new settlement was the local newspaper, the *Cherokee Advocate*, in which Murrell circulated advertisements for his merchandise. By 1844 he was well on his way toward great personal wealth from the sale of woolen muslin, black and green silk, corded skirts, Irish linen, ladies kid and silk gloves, black silk cravats and a rich variety of ribbons and laces.

In 1845 Murrell completed construction on a larger house, situated to the east of the log cabin that greeted his arrival five years earlier. The two-story frame house was nestled amid aging shade trees and was named Hunter's Home after his love for the chase. A short, hipped roof was interrupted at the center of the house where a small gabled extension, resembling a temple pediment, was constructed over a balustraded portico. Slender columns extended from a verranda of equal width on the ground level to brace and adorn the upper portico. The nine-room house was lavishly furnished with articles that had been shipped by river boat to nearby Fort Gibson. Typical of the many pieces, some of which have survived to the present, were a rosewood bedroom suite and sofa. Near the main house, Murrell built a smoke house, a spring house, slave quarters, barns and a mill. There were also extensive orchards within the boundaries of the property.

Murrell's wife died in 1855. Two years later, he married her younger sister and had six children, two of whom died in infancy. Following these personal tragedies, the Civil War erupted and the Indian Territory of Oklahoma became the scene

The Murrell House: Route 82, Tahlequah, Oklahoma. Open to the public.

Above: The Murrell Mansion, constructed in 1845, was the only ante-bellum estate of the prosperous Cherokee Indians to survive marauding Union and Confederate soldiers during the Civil War. Below: Richard Covington was appointed to the U.S. Patent Office in the Grant administration after entertaining the President years before in his log cabin.

of much fighting. Bands of marauding soldiers from both the North and the South criss-crossed the frontier countryside eradicating any trace of antebellum prosperity.

When the destruction of property finally ceased in 1865, the Murrell Mansion was the only building of its particular kind left standing in the entire state. The proud tradition established by the Chero-

kees prior to the war had been all but wiped out in the long years of fighting.

Since that time the Murrell Mansion has been restored and opened to the public as a memorial to an enduring and industrious Cherokee nation. The mansion also recalls the unfortunate repudiation of a people by the Federal Government.

COVINGTON HOUSE
VANCOUVER, WASHINGTON

The Last Frontier

The Covington House is the oldest building in the Vancouver area, one of a few surviving vestiges of an era when the United States was approaching the last of its continental frontiers. Its builder, Richard Covington, was distinguished in his friendship with Ulysses S. Grant, entertaining him at the Vancouver house while he was only a captain and later joining him in Washington, D.C., when he became President.

Built well inland from the Columbia River in 1848, the simple log cabin was suitable for the hardships of the frontier. Unlike the homes of the early French Midwest, the timbers of the Covington House were placed horizontally in an interlocking fashion. The gaps between the logs were filled with a mixture of clay and straw or some similar material. The front of the building has a simple sloping roof with an extension over the entrance supported by two peeled pine logs. The rear roof is longer and cantilever in design. At one end of the house there is a stone chimney which extends the entire height of the building and beyond.

One accompanying outbuilding may have been used as a smoke house. The interior of the house reflects even more the restrained life of these early settlers. Barrenly furnished, the most striking object in the living room is the huge fireplace, capped with a plank mantelpiece almost one foot thick.

Covington first came to Fort Vancouver in 1846, traveling with his wife from his native London, England. As a representative of the Hudson Bay Company, he was to start a school at the fort for the children of the employees. He operated this

school for only two years, receiving during that time an appointment as one of Vancouver's first justices of the peace; then he moved South to take advantage of the Government's land settlement policy. Claiming a site seven miles from Vancouver at Fourth Plains, Covington opened a new school for about two years after building the cabin, boarding young students there at least until 1860.

Aside from his teaching activities, Covington was noted as an artist, musician and inventor among the frontier people. He made numerous sketches and maps of the Vancouver area and later of Oahu Island, Hawaii. He brought the first piano into the Pacific Northwest and once petitioned the patent office in Washington for consideration of a propeller he had developed.

In 1853, Captain Ulysses S. Grant visited Covington, appointing him to head the U.S. Patent Office in 1868. Covington maintained this post throughout the Grant administration, returning to the Northwest in 1877. He stayed there only a year and then traveled to Hawaii, where he died in 1882.

From the time of Covington's departure to Washington, D.C., at the beginning of the Grant administration, his house settled into intermittent periods of abandonment until 1930, when the city of Vancouver dismantled the building and rebuilt it within the city limits. During that same year, the Vancouver Women's Club elected to lease the property as a meeting place and has since maintained the site as a memorial to the diligence with which the first settlers of the Pacific Northwest rolled back the last frontier.

Covington House: W. 39th Street, Vancouver, Washington. Open to the public.

BOWERS MANSION
VIRGINIA CITY, NEVADA

Mrs. Bowers' Melodrama

The story of the Bowers Mansion, a fantastic tale of wealth and desperation, was narrated, years before it occurred, in the crystal ball of Allison Orrum. She was a superstitious farm girl of Scottish descent, obsessed with dreams of great wealth growing out of the impoverishment of her early surroundings. Drawn by visions of Western mountains, criss-crossed by wagon tracks and laboring men, she accompanied her sister and brother-in-law to the Mormon settlement of Nauvoo, Illinois, where she observed in her crystal ball, "I'll have more money than I know what to do with, but I'll be poor again."

Her first impression of the Mormon community was disappointing, but she married one of the elders and, consulting her crystal ball frequently, she accompanied him to Brigham Young's Settlement near the Great Salt Lake. But it soon became evident that her fortune did not lie in the Mormon community. She was unable to have a family and when her newly prosperous husband took on several new wives, her marriage ended.

Finding a younger man whom she felt she could control, "Eilley" Bowers remarried and urged the man to take her to Washoe County, Nevada, near the Comstock. There the mines were belching forth their wealth, but her new husband wasn't interested in forcefully pursuing the fortune that was within reach. Thus when the Mormon settlement again decided to move, Eilley sent her husband along with it, ending her second marriage and she continued her quest alone.

For several months she supported herself at the site of the mines by cooking and washing for the prospectors, until one discouraged miner offered his ten-foot claim in payment of his account. Then, as rapidly as before, she married the man who operated the adjoining claim — Sandy Bowers — and secured her contract with destiny.

The fortune that followed this marriage accumulated at the rate of $18,000 per day at the height of the Comstock boom, and the mansion which was born out of the fortune reflected every extravagance the sudden prosperity could imagine. Originally a huge two-story building surrounded by balustraded porticos on the first and second levels and capped by an adorning rail and cupola on the roof, the house was begun in 1861 and completed in 1864. Stone cutters were imported from Scotland to quarry the marble blocks from the nearby mountains, and so precisely did they work that no mortar was needed to join them. The expansive grounds

Bucket of Blood Saloon, Virginia City, Nevada

Above: Stone cutters imported from Scotland built the Bowers Mansion while Sandy and Eilley Bowers were lifting $18,000 a day from their mines in the Comstock. Years later, Eilley died in a charity home, her fortune dissipated by speculation.

Bowers Mansion: Highway 395, Virginia City, Nevada. Open to the public. Color illustration, p. 186.

were meticulously landscaped and swimming pools were constructed, filled with natural warm water from nearby springs. A fountain in front of the mansion forms a pool which was stocked with goldfish. The lavish furnishings for the house were almost without exception imported from Europe during a year-and-a-half tour, the extravagance of which reputedly overwhelmed the traditional garishness of the *nouveaux riches*.

There were two disappointments during this period of Eilley's life: She was not received by Queen Victoria in England and her great wealth did not attract prominent ladies of society to her entertainments. The death of the only two children born to her might also have caused lasting distress had it not been for the adoption of a girl orphaned by the death of her mother on the return trip from England in 1862. Eilley named this girl Margaret Persia, after her mother and the boat they were traveling on at the time.

The return from Europe, however, also marked a plateau from which all future events would descend. Toward the end of the decade, there was marked concern over production at the Comstock, and in 1868, Sandy died trying to re-establish the mine after the devastation of the previous winter.

While the estate was under settlement, Eilley discovered that their fortune had been drained through the widespread speculation that now threatened the future of the entire Comstock.

In the following years, Eilley attempted to save the house by transforming it into a tourist hotel. Although undaunted by a succession of disappointments in this venture, Eilley was finally crushed by the death of her daughter in 1874. After this, the house was taken from her and she was allowed to live in one of the small cottages on the grounds. Crazed with grief, however, she burned the cottage one night, scorching the Scotch-ivy vines which covered one side of the main house at the same time. She then left the mansion to wander as a clairvoyant, first through Virginia City, then finally to San Francisco where she died in 1903.

The mansion and grounds served as a beer garden through the next 40 years until it was purchased in 1946 by the Reno Women's Civic Club. Restored as authentically as possible, the house and grounds were incorporated into Washoe County as a memorial park to the "Sons and Daughters of Nevada, Veterans of World War II," continuing a tradition of pleasure and recreation that had been foreseen in a crystal ball over 100 years ago.

HEALY HOUSE
LEADVILLE, COLORADO

Gold-Rush Days

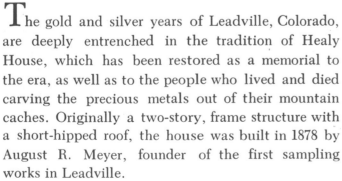

The gold and silver years of Leadville, Colorado, are deeply entrenched in the tradition of Healy House, which has been restored as a memorial to the era, as well as to the people who lived and died carving the precious metals out of their mountain caches. Originally a two-story, frame structure with a short-hipped roof, the house was built in 1878 by August R. Meyer, founder of the first sampling works in Leadville.

The town of Leadville grew out of an earlier mining town that was immediately named Oro City,

when gold was discovered there by a group of discouraged prospectors. They named the site of their strike "California Gulch" and before the year was over, the population of Oro City rose above 10,000. Within five years, the hordes of miners who followed after the original strike lifted $3,000,000 out of California Gulch.

This first population of Oro City was transient. Gold seekers, entertainers, gamblers, each was bent only on the wealth promised in the jagged hills which overlooked the booming settlement. However,

Healy House State Historical Monument: 912 Harrison Avenue, Leadville, Colo. Open to the public. Color illus., p. 185.